ON THE NATURE OF THE UNIVERSE
DE RERUM NATURA
BOOK 1

— *Lucretius* —
ON THE NATURE OF THE UNIVERSE
DE RERUM NATURA
BOOK 1

Translated
and with a Preface by
EMMA GEE

Published by Arc Publications,
Nanholme Mill, Shaw Wood Road
Todmorden OL14 6DA, UK
www.arcpublications.co.uk

Translation copyright © Emma Gee, 2020
Translator's Preface copyright © Emma Gee, 2020
Copyright in the present edition © Arc Publications, 2020

978 1908376 08 4 (pbk)
978 1908376 96 1 (ebk)

ACKNOWLEDGEMENTS

The translator would like to thank her son Hal for his critical comments and IT help, her friend Gillian Galbraith for reading the poem in draft, Jo Balmer for her unstinting encouragement and, for their careful reading and editing, Arc's Translations Editor Jean Boase-Beier and Arc Editor Angela Jarman.

Design by Tony Ward

Cover picture:
'The winged Fury' detail of the dionysiac frieze, painted mural, Villa dei Misteri, Pompei, II Pompeian style (I century BC). Reproduced with the permission of Ministero per i Beni e le Attività Culturali / Archivi Alinari, Firenze

This book is copyright. Subject to statutory exception and to provisions of relevant collective licensing agreements, no reproduction of any part of this book may take place without the written permission of Arc Publications Ltd.

This book has been selected to receive financial assistance from English PEN's 'PEN Translates' programme, supported by Arts Council England. PEN exists to promote literature and our understanding of it, to uphold writers' freedoms around the world, to campaign against the persecution and imprisonment of writers for stating their views, and to promote the friendly co-operation of writers and the free exchange of ideas.
www.englishpen.org

'Arc Publications Classics: New Translations
of Great Poets of the Past'
Series Editor: Jean Boase-Beier

In memory of Robin

*who told me to write something
people could understand*

CONTENTS

Translator's Preface / 9

1 Venus / 15
2 The Gods Don't Care / 18
3 Lucretius' Programme / 20
4 Epicurus / 22
5 Human Sacrifice / 24
6 False Prophets / 26
7 Translation / 29
8 Nothing Comes from Nothing / 30
9 Nothing Dissolves into Nothing / 35
10 Unseen Bodies / 40
11 Void / 46
12 Examples of Void / 50
13 Endless Possibilities for Proof / 53
14 Void, Continued / 55
15 Time / 58
16 Matter is Solid, Separate, Eternal / 61
17 Atoms Can't Be Cut / 71
18 Deluded Theories 1: Heraclitus / 74
19 Deluded Theories 2: Empedocles / 81
20 Deluded Theories 3: Anaxagoras / 91
21 Lucretius' Aim / 99
22 The Universe is Infinite / 102
23 There is No Middle / 110
24 The Way of Truth / 114

Biographical Notes / 115

TRANSLATOR'S PREFACE

...Lucretius' doctrine seems unpalatable
if you haven't tasted it
people are revolted by it
as by some strange smelly fruit
his Latin is difficult, impenetrable to most
not just because it's Latin
but because of what it says...

    Lucretius, *On the Nature of the Universe* 1. 943-45

Lucretius is a difficult poet; translating, even reading, his *De rerum natura* (On the Nature of the Universe), has been fraught with perils since the time of writing in c. 55 BCE. The poem is brutally reductionist. Lucretius' explorations of cosmology, psychology, anthropology and astronomy reflect Greek science as understood by his intellectual model Epicurus (341-270 BCE). The Epicurean system of physics encompassed everything, from the quantum to the very large; from the nature of the human psyche to the physics of colour. Its foundation was one of extreme materialism. The world as we perceive it is a product of two things only: atoms and space (or, as we call them here, Body and Void). Lucretius is also an atheist, of a kind. The gods, if they exist, have no role in cosmic or human affairs; they stand as symbols of supreme detachment (*ataraxia*).

  Detachment was necessary for Lucretius. Although he is evasive about events which are taking place at the time of writing, Lucretius was witnessing the dissolution of the longstanding Republican system of government, and the nascent political strife which would develop into civil war and finally totalitarian rule. Lucretius tears apart the familiar universe at the end of Book 1; this mirrors the collapse of political certainties in the late Roman Republic.

  Lucretius' text walks in step with difficult times. It was a woman, Lucy Hutchinson, who made the first full English translation of the *De rerum natura* in the 1650s, during the interregnum, that fluid and dangerous period after the English civil war. In her dedication to the Earl of Anglesey, written in 1675, she, like Lucretius at the beginning of his poem (see no. 2), laments the time she lived in. Lucy casts her era as a jeering mob, 'this drolling degenerate age, that hath hisst out all sober and serious studies'.

Lucy saw her translation of Lucretius as a moral battle. To read Lucretius' atheistic poem was (in her words), 'a wanton dalliance with impious bookes.' Only through inside knowledge of the poem by translation could Lucy avoid (as it were) intellectual adultery. She portrays Lucretius' atoms as Restoration libertines, dancing feathered and coiffed, showily antipathetic to seventeeth-century Puritan restraint:

> Tis a lamentation and horror, that in these days of the Gospell, Men should be found so presumptuously wicked, to studie & adhere to his & his masters ridiculous, impious, execrable doctrines, reviving the foppish casuall dance of attoms...

Lucy is onto something here. Flamboyant and subversive Lucretius' poem certainly is; accomplished in its techniques of persuasion, furious in its attacks on conformity. This is probably why the poem was nearly lost to us altogether. There's no evidence that anyone between the tenth century, the time of our earliest manuscripts, and the rediscovery of the text in 1417 read it, although lack of evidence doesn't necessarily mean it was off the menu: the *De rerum natura* isn't a work that a monastery would happily have inscribed in its catalogues. Monks read it, if they did, under the radar. After its Renaissance rediscovery the *De rerum natura* exerted a dangerous fascination, as of a powerful psychoactive drug. Thus also its fascination and repulsion for Lucy Hutchinson.

Lucretius' poem can – and should – still provoke

extreme reactions. Lucretius' cosmos is a callous and emotionless place, not designed to foster human life. The poem ends with the wholesale destruction of the human race by a pandemic, described in unflinching detail. Lucretius' writing, too, is deliberately offensive. The poet challenges us, calls us stupid, bores us with repetitions, makes us hoot with laughter, provokes indignation, shame, anxiety. This is not so much because we see the embryo of contemporary thought in him, although this is also true, as because we still *feel*.

Yet authentic experience of Lucretius' text remains largely inaccessible, not just to the non-Latinist, but even to those Latinists who have not taken a lengthy bath in the glacial waters of textual criticism, that forbidding ecosystem populated by a dark fauna of *sigla* and *apparatus critici*.

This translation is intended for everyone, the curious and the scholarly alike. It's my job as a translator not just to sketch in the iceberg under the tip, but to give Lucretius back his mischief. I describe my translation of Lucretius as a mirror ball – something exciting, glittering, fractured (see no. 7). I've been ruthless in exerting the traction of modernity on the poem: I update Lucretius' images in ways some may criticise as anachronistic; others may find the friction between ancient and modern pleasurable. 'Anarchic Aphrodite' (no. 1) borrows from the final passage of W. H. Auden's 'In Memory of Sigmund Freud'; the 'selfish gene' alludes to the work of Richard Dawkins. These allusions provide psychoanalytic and biological 'keys' to the goddess Venus, whose presence in Lucretius' 'atheistic' poem has long posed a problem for scholars. Aldous Huxley appears in no. 19, 'the doors / between perception and conjecture'. Lucretius' poem is – literally – psychedelic: it strips away religion and shows us the human soul as a material entity, coextensive with the material universe. R. D. Laing puts in an appearance in the final line of no. 1, where Venus becomes the fulfilment of his wish at the end of *The Bird of Paradise* ('If I could turn you on, if I could drive you out of your wretched mind...'). I give Lucretius a microscope (no. 20); his 'honeyed cup' of poetry becomes the polio vaccine (no. 21). I turn myth, foreign to the modern reader, into allegory. So the myth of the Trojan Horse (no. 15) becomes in my text a metaphor for the pernicious tendency of history to spawn ideologies.

Mine is an account of the first book of Lucretius' poem which strives to reproduce the sonic and linguistic effects of the Latin, in a form which can be grasped by users of smartphones. I have tried to convey the roughness of Lucretius' sound-world; I have retained his formulae and repetitions. I have both embraced and resisted the urge of English to dissolve into iambic pentameters, creating a tension both towards and away from order, in a way which mirrors the contrary forces at work in the explosive world of the *De rerum natura*.

NOTE ON THE EDITIONS USED

The Latin text is taken from the online Latin Library, with readings modified as necessary to reconcile it with the edition I used, namely Cyril Bailey's 1900 *Oxford Classical Text*. My translation was complete prior to the appearance of Marcus Deufert's 2019 Teubner edition. I have however followed Deufert in restoring *DRN* 1.44-49.

Emma Gee

FURTHER READING

Bailey, C., *Lucreti de rerum natura libri sex* (second edition), Oxford: Clarendon Press, 1900.
Barbour, R., and Norbrook, D. , *The Works of Lucy Hutchinson Volume 1: the Translation of Lucretius*, parts 1 & 2, Oxford: Oxford University Press, 2012.
Butterfield, D., *The Early Textual History of Lucretius' De rerum natura*, Cambridge: Cambridge University Press, 2013.
Deufert, M., *Titus Lucretius Carus:* De rerum natura *libri VI*, Berlin: De Gruyter, 2019.
Greenblatt, S., *The Swerve: How the Renaissance Began*, New York: Norton, 2011.
Greer, G. et al., *Kissing the Rod: an Anthology of Seventeenth Century Women's Verse,* New York: Farrar Straus Giroux, c. 1988.
Stallings, A. E., *Lucretius: the Nature of Things*, Penguin, 2007.

1 VENUS (1-40)

Imagine there's a god
a goddess even
let's call her the Goddess of Love
no Botticelli Venus climbing out of a shell
but Nature – anarchic Aphrodite
she builds things up then kicks them
down again like an angry toddler.

the selfish gene, the pleasure principle
she fills to brim the ship-enduring sea
crop-heavy earth; coaxes every living thing
beneath the sliding signs of heaven
to leap into the light.

the clouds scud escort when she comes
Architect Earth throws down the red carpet
the mirror sea blinks back the smiling sky.

she flings the veil from day's Spring face
slides back the bolts which stall the winds
shoots down the little birds midair
each one a sounding bell
struck through the heart
the whole dawn chorus a reckless
cascade of notes tumbling
mi-re-do
down from above.

bent on increase she
goads every species wild or tame
to buck the winter off
cross seas and mountains
ford foamy rivers

follow where libido leads
in an orgy of replication.

you too: she'll flatter you
into thinking you're in love; seduce you
with cotton-wool clouds and lambs
lull you with soft summer –

then she'll say: 'Think you can come at me
with your dragnets and carbon footprint?
I'll truss your machismo up
and crack your neck till you beg for mercy.'

can this dominatrix turn our wars to love?
of course, for she rules all.
without her no sun would ever rise
above the holy borderlands of light.

so she's the god I'd call
to beat my song's bronze gong:
the tart who starts the music,
turns the stars, turns you on.

>   Aeneadum genetrix, hominum divumque voluptas,
>   alma Venus, caeli subter labentia signa
>   quae mare navigerum, quae terras frugiferentis
>   concelebras, per te quoniam genus omne animantum
>   concipitur visitque exortum lumina solis: 5
>   te, dea, te fugiunt venti, te nubila caeli
>   adventumque tuum, tibi suavis daedala tellus
>   summittit flores, tibi rident aequora ponti
>   placatumque nitet diffuso lumine caelum.
>   nam simul ac species patefactast verna diei   10

et reserata viget genitabilis aura favoni,
aeriae primum volucres te, diva, tuumque
significant initum perculsae corda tua vi.
inde ferae pecudes persultant pabula laeta   [15]
et rapidos tranant amnis: ita capta lepore   15 [14]
te sequitur cupide quo quamque inducere pergis.
denique per maria ac montis fluviosque rapaces
frondiferasque domos avium camposque virentis
omnibus incutiens blandum per pectora amorem
efficis ut cupide generatim saecla propagent.   20
quae quoniam rerum naturam sola gubernas
nec sine te quicquam dias in luminis oras
exoritur neque fit laetum neque amabile quicquam,
te sociam studeo scribendis versibus esse
quos ego de rerum natura pangere conor   25
Memmiadae nostro, quem tu, dea, tempore in omni
omnibus ornatum voluisti excellere rebus.
quo magis aeternum da dictis, diva, leporem.
effice ut interea fera moenera militiai
per maria ac terras omnis sopita quiescant.   30
nam tu sola potes tranquilla pace iuvare
mortalis, quoniam belli fera moenera Mavors
armipotens regit, in gremium qui saepe tuum se
reicit aeterno devictus vulnere amoris,
atque ita suspiciens tereti cervice reposta   35
pascit amore avidos inhians in te, dea, visus
eque tuo pendet resupini spiritus ore.
hunc tu, diva, tuo recubantem corpore sancto
circumfusa super, suavis ex ore loquelas
funde petens placidam Romanis, incluta, pacem.   40

2 THE GODS DON'T CARE (41-9)

How can I complete this task
when the limits of what's human
are defined by walls of hate
and self-devised destruction?
how can any saviour of the state
look past the slogans they misjudge
to be the boundaries of the universe
and see the view beyond?

if the gods cared about mankind
they wouldn't be the gods.
this is their rationale:
they live forever
walled around by class
they feel no grief
no pain; they are immune
to ordinary dangers
untouchable
fat-cats lolling in some
divinely sanctioned
chardonnay-sipping
heavenly tax-haven.
they have no need of us
they're not seduced by promises
or moved by our resentment.

> nam neque nos agere hoc patriai tempore iniquo
> possumus aequo animo nec Memmi clara propago
> talibus in rebus communi desse saluti.
> {omnis enim per se divum natura necessest

immortali aevo summa cum pace fruatur 45
semota ab nostris rebus seiunctaque longe.
nam privata dolore omni, privata periclis,
ipsa suis pollens opibus, nihil indiga nostri,
nec bene promeritis capitur nec tangitur ira.}

3 LUCRETIUS' PROGRAMME (50-61)

Save yourself:
open your ears
find some headspace
turn to truth.
don't turn your nose up
at the gifts I bring
before you've understood them.

I will unpick the threads of heaven
and disrobe the gods for you;
I'll rip open the skin of the universe
and show its guts
the raw material that
what we call Nature
uses to make the shapes of things
we think we know;
raises them, compels them
to grow, and once things die
how that same Nature liquidates
what's left into the primal stuff
that we call Matter, Life-force,
the Seed of Things;
by the power of reason
I'll boil it down
to something we can understand:
First Bodies, the foundations of the universe.

       quod superest, vacuas auris <animumque sagacem> 50
       semotum a curis adhibe veram ad rationem,
       ne mea dona tibi studio disposta fideli,
       intellecta prius quam sint, contempta relinquas.
       nam tibi de summa caeli ratione deumque
       disserere incipiam et rerum primordia pandam, 55

unde omnis natura creet res auctet alatque
quove eadem rursum natura perempta resolvat,
quae nos materiem et genitalia corpora rebus
reddunda in ratione vocare et semina rerum
appellare suemus et haec eadem usurpare 60
corpora prima, quod ex illis sunt omnia primis.

4 EPICURUS (62-79)

Humanity lay grovelling
religion our hallucination
until a Greek stood across the path
where its shadow fell.

he wasn't cowed by heaven's tantrums
they just fired him up
to want to be the first to smash open
the bolts on nature's doors

a stuntman blasting through
the world's walls of fire
his orbit looped the universe
the sheer bravado of his intellect won out

he came back with the prize
of knowing –
knowing what forms things can take
what's impossible
why the limitations

he found the boundary-stone of the cosmos
its foot sunk deep
he ground religion's stub beneath his heel
and made humanity tall as the sky.

> humana ante oculos foede cum vita iaceret
> in terris oppressa gravi sub religione
> quae caput a caeli regionibus ostendebat
> horribili super aspectu mortalibus instans,   65
> primum Graius homo mortalis tollere contra
> est oculos ausus primusque obsistere contra,
> quem neque fama deum nec fulmina nec minitanti

murmure compressit caelum, sed eo magis acrem
irritat animi virtutem, effringere ut arta 70
naturae primus portarum claustra cupiret.
ergo vivida vis animi pervicit, et extra
processit longe flammantia moenia mundi
atque omne immensum peragravit mente animoque,
unde refert nobis victor quid possit oriri, 75
quid nequeat, finita potestas denique cuique
quanam sit ratione atque alte terminus haerens.
quare religio pedibus subiecta vicissim
obteritur, nos exaequat victoria caelo.

5 HUMAN SACRIFICE (80-101)

You think I'll make you ride
the slippery slope of
moral relaxation where
without religious scruples for brakes
anything goes.

far from it. time and again
religion spawns atrocities.

in a world where people send their children out
in suicide belts or camouflage
don't think we've come so far
it's just the same as when
Greathearted Heroes of the Greeks
made the altar of Trivia slippery
with the blood of that young girl –
Iphianissa –

when the victim's headband trickled
like tears down her cheeks
and she saw her father standing by the altar
grieving already
next to him the priest
hiding a blade
the crowd shedding tears at the look of her:
she fell to her knees in mute appeal.

it didn't count in her favour
that she was the first to give the king a father's name:
she was led trembling to the altar
not given away in the company
of the bright-robed God of Couples
but subdued by a yoke of male hands
a sad offering felled in place of marriage

by her father, the murderer
– shame on him! – an insurance policy
for the success of Greek ships.
This is the scale of crime religion paints as right.

    illud in his rebus vereor, ne forte rearis   80
impia te rationis inire elementa viamque
indugredi sceleris. quod contra saepius illa
religio peperit scelerosa atque impia facta.
Aulide quo pacto Triviai virginis aram
Iphianassai turparunt sanguine foede   85
ductores Danaum delecti, prima virorum.
cui simul infula virgineos circumdata comptus
ex utraque pari malarum parte profusast,
et maestum simul ante aras adstare parentem
sensit et hunc propter ferrum celare ministros   90
aspectuque suo lacrimas effundere civis,
muta metu terram genibus summissa petebat.
nec miserae prodesse in tali tempore quibat
quod patrio princeps donarat nomine regem.
nam sublata virum manibus tremibundaque ad aras 95
deductast, non ut sollemni more sacrorum
perfecto posset claro comitari Hymenaeo,
sed casta inceste nubendi tempore in ipso
hostia concideret mactatu maesta parentis,
exitus ut classi felix faustusque daretur.   100
tantum religio potuit suadere malorum.

6 FALSE PROPHETS (102-135)

I know you'll cancel your appointment with the truth:
it's so much easier to accept
the sentence tradition hands down.

those seductive evangelists
turn your life upside-down
with delusions crafted just for you
paralyse you with fear
so any self-directed move becomes impossible.

how right they are!

for if it looked as though we could point precisely
to the end of human suffering
we'd tell the gurus where to get off.

the Afterlife conspiracy serves them well:
it's in their interest to make sure it continues
so we can't see an end to the degradation of our lives.

they get away with it
because we don't understand
what the soul is –
innate or inserted during birth –
whether it dies, split off from us
and sees vast shadowlands below
or whether by Divine Hand
it sniffs about the animal kingdom
looking for another body to curl itself
up in.

this was what Ennius said – our oldest poet –
when he shouldered the Muses' mantle

borrowed from craggy Greece
put on a wreath of no deciduous leaf
so we Romans remember him always.

but he made no sense –
for all the same he told us
in the everlasting circles of his words
that there's a city underground
even though we don't find our souls or bodies there
but some near-diaphanous double.

he even told how Homer
like an everlasting flower
rose up from there
and – cheeks salt with emotion –
started to proclaim the nature of the universe.

this powerful rubbish motivates us
to look to reason as regards the Things Above –
the mechanism that drives the sun's path
the moon's meanderings
why things happen here on earth –

above all to scrutinize the source from which the Self
and the nub of the intelligence are put together
the nightmares which hunt us down
and take away our ability to think
when, awake, we're in the grip of some psychosis
or when we're buried in sleep
and the dead come to us,
alive, in face and voice –
dreams and visions
of those whose bones earth holds in her embrace.

tutemet a nobis iam quovis tempore vatum
terriloquis victus dictis desciscere quaeres.
quippe etenim quam multa tibi iam fingere possunt
somnia quae vitae rationes vertere possint 105
fortunasque tuas omnis turbare timore!
et merito. nam si certam finem esse viderent
aerumnarum homines, aliqua ratione valerent
religionibus atque minis obsistere vatum.
nunc ratio nulla est restandi, nulla facultas, 110
aeternas quoniam poenas in morte timendumst.
ignoratur enim quae sit natura animai,
nata sit an contra nascentibus insinuetur,
et simul intereat nobiscum morte dirempta
an tenebras Orci visat vastasque lacunas 115
an pecudes alias divinitus insinuet se,
Ennius ut noster cecinit qui primus amoeno
detulit ex Helicone perenni fronde coronam,
per gentis Italas hominum quae clara clueret;
etsi praeterea tamen esse Acherusia templa 120
Ennius aeternis exponit versibus edens,
quo neque permaneant animae neque corpora nostra,
sed quaedam simulacra modis pallentia miris;
unde sibi exortam semper florentis Homeri
commemorat speciem lacrimas effundere salsas 125
coepisse et rerum naturam expandere dictis.
quapropter bene cum superis de rebus habenda
nobis est ratio, solis lunaeque meatus
qua fiant ratione, et qua vi quaeque gerantur
in terris, tunc cum primis ratione sagaci 130
unde anima atque animi constet natura videndum,
et quae res nobis vigilantibus obvia mentis
terrificet morbo adfectis somnoque sepultis,
cernere uti videamur eos audireque coram,
morte obita quorum tellus amplectitur ossa. 135

7 TRANSLATION (136-145)

Sometimes it seems impossible
I'm too tongue-tied, the material's too controversial
it's too difficult to make Lucretius' Latin shine
when monosyllables are practically all
that Anglo-Saxon has to offer –

but then I think of you, my dearest friend,
your stubbornness in the face of the impossible
and I hope to make you like me more
by living up to your standards.

all this keeps me awake in the traffic-free night
turning each word this way and that
trying to find a way
to spin the mirrorball towards the light
so its refractive points reveal for you
the deep-buried mosaic of the universe.

    nec me animi fallit Graiorum obscura reperta
    difficile inlustrare Latinis versibus esse,
    multa novis verbis praesertim cum sit agendum
    propter egestatem linguae et rerum novitatem;
    sed tua me virtus tamen et sperata voluptas   140
    suavis amicitiae quemvis efferre laborem
    suadet et inducit noctes vigilare serenas
    quaerentem dictis quibus et quo carmine demum
    clara tuae possim praepandere lumina menti,
    res quibus occultas penitus convisere possis.   145

8 NOTHING COMES FROM NOTHING (146-214)

The sun's weapons, brittle lances of light
can't scatter the mind's black horrors:
only if we peel open nature and look in.
then we'll see there's no Divine Hand
birthing something from nothing.

once you see that nothing comes from nothing
then you'll understand how all things come together,
arise, continue to exist, without a god.
if beings came from nothing,
if anything could give birth to anything
humans would flower from the sea,
fish shake their scales free of earth
birds rain from the air like technicolour satellite debris;
sheep and cows and every wild species
would pour promiscuously out
to colonize farmland and wilderness alike;
trees would not bear fruit according to type
but change and change about.

without genetic blueprint
nature would be one big commune
where no child knows its birth mother.
but nature to all things
gives templates for their growth
places them at the starting-gate
to cross by a specific route
the checkpoint to the land of light.

things can't give rise
to infinite varieties of other things: instead
there's a secret proclivity in everything
for what it must become.

why else, say, does earth with a casual flourish
magic rills of roses from Spring, corn from Summer
why do grapes tumesce under Autumn's gentle hand

if not because the unique identity of things
follows the Diktat of their creation
and lines them up at times best suited to their welfare
to cross the checkpoint to the land of light?

but if things came from nothing,
they'd spring up unpredictably
and at the wrong time of year
without the seeds which join
in fruitful conflux
at a time designed to flout the odds.

people would not need the space to grow
from conception to adulthood:
toddlers would leap straight to puberty
saplings spring ready-plumed from the ground.

it's clear this doesn't happen:
we grow up properly, bit by bit
each species faithful to its own intent
and each in need of timely rain or food
to achieve its predetermined self –
the genetic word in tangible form.

not only does matter provide instructions for assembly
but it puts a stop to excess growth as well.
the superhero is impossible –
men can't stride the sea like a wading pool
hold mountains up, roots dangling

or outlive centuries –
why else than because matter is tailored
to the making of specific things?

everything needs seeds unique to it:
not one thing exhaled on gentle breath of air
comes from nowhere.

if you want final proof
that there are seeds invisible to sight
take the fact that places worked
respond more generously to human hand
when we coax seeds through stifling cowl of earth
we've perforated by the share.
if seeds weren't already present in the earth
designed to be receptive to the plough
it wouldn't help to bring them to the light:
things would grow much better by themselves.

> hunc igitur terrorem animi tenebrasque necessest
> non radii solis neque lucida tela diei
> discutiant, sed naturae species ratioque.
> principium cuius hinc nobis exordia sumet,
> nullam rem e nihilo gigni divinitus umquam. 150
> quippe ita formido mortalis continet omnis,
> quod multa in terris fieri caeloque tuentur
> quorum operum causas nulla ratione videre
> possunt ac fieri divino numine rentur.
> quas ob res ubi viderimus nil posse creari 155 [156]
> de nilo, tum quod sequimur iam rectius inde [157]
> perspiciemus, et unde queat res quaeque creari [158]
> et quo quaeque modo fiant opera sine divum. [155]
> nam si de nihilo fierent, ex omnibu' rebus

omne genus nasci posset, nil semine egeret. 160
e mare primum homines, e terra posset oriri
squamigerum genus et volucres erumpere caelo;
armenta atque aliae pecudes, genus omne ferarum,
incerto partu culta ac deserta tenerent.
nec fructus idem arboribus constare solerent, 165
sed mutarentur, ferre omnes omnia possent.
quippe ubi non essent genitalia corpora cuique,
qui posset mater rebus consistere certa?
at nunc seminibus quia certis quaeque creantur,
inde enascitur atque oras in luminis exit, 170
materies ubi inest cuiusque et corpora prima;
atque hac re nequeunt ex omnibus omnia gigni,
quod certis in rebus inest secreta facultas.
praeterea cur vere rosam, frumenta calore,
vitis autumno fundi suadente videmus, 175
si non, certa suo quia tempore semina rerum
cum confluxerunt, patefit quod cumque creatur,
dum tempestates adsunt et vivida tellus
tuto res teneras effert in luminis oras?
quod si de nihilo fierent, subito exorerentur 180
incerto spatio atque alienis partibus anni,
quippe ubi nulla forent primordia quae genitali
concilio possent arceri tempore iniquo.
nec porro augendis rebus spatio foret usus
seminis ad coitum, si e nilo crescere possent. 185
nam fierent iuvenes subito ex infantibu' parvis
e terraque exorta repente arbusta salirent.
quorum nil fieri manifestum est, omnia quando
paulatim crescunt, ut par est, semine certo
crescentesque genus servant; ut noscere possis 190
quidque sua de materia grandescere alique.
huc accedit uti sine certis imbribus anni
laetificos nequeat fetus submittere tellus

nec porro secreta cibo natura animantum
propagare genus possit vitamque tueri; 195
ut potius multis communia corpora rebus
multa putes esse, ut verbis elementa videmus,
quam sine principiis ullam rem existere posse.
denique cur homines tantos natura parare
non potuit, pedibus qui pontum per vada possent 200
transire et magnos manibus divellere montis
multaque vivendo vitalia vincere saecla,
si non, materies quia rebus reddita certast
gignundis e qua constat quid possit oriri?
nil igitur fieri de nilo posse fatendumst, 205
semine quando opus est rebus quo quaeque creatae
aeris in teneras possint proferrier auras.
postremo quoniam incultis praestare videmus
culta loca et manibus melioris reddere fetus,
esse videlicet in terris primordia rerum 210
quae nos fecundas vertentes vomere glebas
terraique solum subigentes cimus ad ortus.
quod si nulla forent, nostro sine quaeque labore
sponte sua multo fieri meliora videres.

9 NOTHING DISSOLVES INTO NOTHING (215-264)

Nothing is obliterated
things just resolve into their constituents.

if stuff was made only of parts which die
then death would be a conjuring trick –
there'd be no struggle
no need for forceful sundering of
alliances between components.

as it is
nature brooks no destruction of the assemblage
except if smashed
by blow on blow from outside
or when some force gets in the space inside
strong enough to prise the particles apart.

if time brought total annihilation
eating things away right down to the core
gorging on every last bit of matter
what would be left for Venus to work with?
where would she start, to tempt
living things out one by one into the light?
how would Architect Earth
feed and raise her adoptees
offering them the right titbits one by one?

from what far source
would free-born burns
come to fatten the sea?
how would the sky pasture the stars?

if our smallest components were capable of dying
everything would have been used up by now.
but if for unimaginable time some entities exist
from which the structure of the whole
is continually rebuilt –
those things would be immune to death for sure
since matter can't be lost.

the same causes
would wreak destruction nearly always
if matter wasn't constant,
held more or less
tightly in temporary ties.

unless the threads of matter were
designed to be unpicked by force precise to each,
one caress of death's soft fingers
would unlace their fabric.

as it is, while matter lives forever
though its colours are expressed in different weaves
entities don't unravel
until they meet with that degree of tearing
adapted to their weft.

even then they don't degrade to nil –
everything just resolves into its Primary Parts.

the raindrops Father Sky casts
in the womb of Mother Earth
these seem to die, but then we see
the shining spikes of crops
prick through the land;
the neon green of foliage

lights up the branches
the trees stoop down to give us fruit –
us and the beasts.
from this source we see cities
put forth their flowers of children
from here the woods' uncurling fronds
sing all about with voices of new birds;
herds make a lying-place in crushed grass
tired of schlepping their fat about
leave a stamp of themselves
upon the richness of their fodder
their tight udders release a snowy
freefall of milk drops.
from this source too their newborn calves
lurch across green velvet fields
on crazy limbs, trying to play
high on milk too pure for their tiny minds.
nothing that we see perishes deep down
nature replenishes every living thing
from another's death:
nothing dies that doesn't gift a life.

    huc accedit uti quidque in sua corpora rursum   215
    dissoluat natura neque ad nihilum interimat res.
    nam si quid mortale \<e\> cunctis partibus esset,
    ex oculis res quaeque repente erepta periret.
    nulla vi foret usus enim quae partibus eius
    discidium parere et nexus exsolvere posset.   220
    quod nunc, aeterno quia constant semine quaeque,
    donec vis obiit quae res diverberet ictu
    aut intus penetret per inania dissoluatque,
    nullius exitium patitur natura videri.
    praeterea quaecumque vetustate amovet aetas,   225

si penitus peremit consumens materiem omnem,
unde animale genus generatim in lumina vitae
redducit Venus, aut redductum daedala tellus
unde alit atque auget generatim pabula praebens?
unde mare ingenui fontes externaque longe   230
flumina suppeditant? unde aether sidera pascit?
omnia enim debet, mortali corpore quae sunt,
infinita aetas consumpse anteacta diesque.
quod si in eo spatio atque anteacta aetate fuere
e quibus haec rerum consistit summa refecta,   235
immortali sunt natura praedita certe;
haud igitur possunt ad nilum quaeque reverti.
denique res omnis eadem vis causaque vulgo
conficeret, nisi materies aeterna teneret,
inter se nexu minus aut magis indupedita.   240
tactus enim leti satis esset causa profecto,
quippe ubi nulla forent aeterno corpore quorum
contextum vis deberet dissolvere quaeque.
at nunc, inter se quia nexus principiorum
dissimiles constant aeternaque materies est,   245
incolumi remanent res corpore, dum satis acris
vis obeat pro textura cuiusque reperta.
haud igitur redit ad nihilum res ulla, sed omnes
discidio redeunt in corpora materiai.
postremo pereunt imbres, ubi eos pater aether   250
in gremium matris terrai praecipitavit;
at nitidae surgunt fruges ramique virescunt
arboribus, crescunt ipsae fetuque gravantur;
hinc alitur porro nostrum genus atque ferarum,
hinc laetas urbes pueris florere videmus   255
frondiferasque novis avibus canere undique silvas;
hinc fessae pecudes pingui per pabula laeta
corpora deponunt et candens lacteus umor
uberibus manat distentis; hinc nova proles

artubus infirmis teneras lasciva per herbas   260
ludit lacte mero mentis perculsa novellas.
haud igitur penitus pereunt quaecumque videntur,
quando alid ex alio reficit natura nec ullam
rem gigni patitur nisi morte adiuta aliena.

10 UNSEEN BODIES (265-328)

I've taught that things aren't made from nothing
or, once made, revoked to nothingness.

but just in case you brand my words
as much an act of faith
as those religious ramblings I decry
because the Primary Bodies can't be seen –
think about phenomena
whose only explanation lies in unseen particles.
first among these is wind.
wind's whirling lashes white horses
swoops on ships
rips clouds like kids pull fairy floss apart

other times
it builds up to a rant from threatening mutter
courses plains, a lethal spinning cone
or wraps around the woods
and when it leaves
the hills are dressed in matchstick tresses
like Mount St Helens
just by force of air.

wind's matter, dark to sight
sweeps like a massive broom
the sea, sweeps earth, sweeps
the clouds of heaven even,
snatching them in sudden eddy –

wind is like a river
only one you can't see.
its unseen forces
proliferate destruction by impulse
just as when water's gentle nature

suddenly turns nasty
when rain upstream
brings about a personality shift;
a mountain-fed apocalypse
measuring its pressure in tens of tons
grabs whole chunks of forest, little islands
with mini plantations riding on them;
grinds boulders in its way
like ball bearings
then hurls them down
a lethal Niagara;
brushes ancient bridges aside
with a dismissive gesture
and spreads destruction's effluent everywhere.

gusts of wind have to behave the same:
with the same muscle as a river
they fall upon locations at their whim
propel things before their breath's rocket thrust
snatch them up where caprice takes them;
build a crazy tower which walks the earth
poised in gravity-defying slow motion
whilst at its core a hungry vortex
whirls too fast for the eye to see.

with equal force
my reiterated hammer blows of proof
break open wind's matter dark to sight
till we see it engaged in underhanded emulation
of acts which in rivers are overt.

think too about smells:
smells that trigger different associations
although we don't see anything coming to our nose.

we can't grasp hot and cold
we can't see voices
and yet they must have bodily components
because they can impact upon our senses
through the finger-brush of atoms.

waves of washing strung up near the beach
suck up water, then dry out
when you spread their billows in the sun;
though there's no way of seeing how
the water-particles settle on them
or how they dissipate with heat.
water's distilled in drops
too small for the eye to see.

the sun's advance and retreat across the year
thins a ring's underside just by wearing
drop-fall hollows rocks
the ploughshare shrinks in secret
in the dirt of the fields;
we see in ancient streets
a channel carved by feet of generations;
or a statue, foot thinned to a wisp
by the stroking of countless
passers through the ancient doors he guards

but nature doesn't let us see
which bodies are subtracted
or how or when.

our eyes' bright shaft can't penetrate
whatever nature allocates in daily ration
causing things to grow bit by bit
or when they diminish

through time's emaciation;
although we see an overhang of rock
which the sea boils up under
licked away by salt,
we can't sequence the process of attrition.

so nature animates the universe by bodies dark to sight.

nunc age, res quoniam docui non posse creari 265
de nilo neque item genitas ad nil revocari,
nequa forte tamen coeptes diffidere dictis,
quod nequeunt oculis rerum primordia cerni,
accipe praeterea quae corpora tute necessest
confiteare esse in rebus nec posse videri. 270
principio venti vis verberat incita pontum
ingentisque ruit navis et nubila differt,
interdum rapido percurrens turbine campos
arboribus magnis sternit montisque supremos
silvifragis vexat flabris: ita perfurit acri 275
cum fremitu saevitque minaci murmure ventus.
sunt igitur venti nimirum corpora caeca
quae mare, quae terras, quae denique nubila caeli
verrunt ac subito vexantia turbine raptant,
nec ratione fluunt alia stragemque propagant 280
et cum mollis aquae fertur natura repente
flumine abundanti, quam largis imbribus auget
montibus ex altis magnus decursus aquai
fragmina coniciens silvarum arbustaque tota,
nec validi possunt pontes venientis aquai 285
vim subitam tolerare: ita magno turbidus imbri
molibus incurrit validis cum viribus amnis.
dat sonitu magno stragem volvitque sub undis
grandia saxa ruit †qua quidquid† fluctibus obstat.

sic igitur debent venti quoque flamina ferri, 290
quae veluti validum cum flumen procubuere
quamlibet in partem, trudunt res ante ruuntque
impetibus crebris, interdum vertice torto
corripiunt rapideque rotanti turbine portant.
quare etiam atque etiam sunt venti corpora caeca, 295
quandoquidem factis et moribus aemula magnis
amnibus inveniuntur, aperto corpore qui sunt.
tum porro varios rerum sentimus odores
nec tamen ad naris venientis cernimus umquam,
nec calidos aestus tuimur nec frigora quimus 300
usurpare oculis nec voces cernere suemus;
quae tamen omnia corporea constare necessest
natura, quoniam sensus inpellere possunt.
tangere enim et tangi, nisi corpus, nulla potest res.
denique fluctifrago suspensae in litore vestis 305
uvescunt, eaedem dispansae in sole serescunt.
at neque quo pacto persederit umor aquai
visumst nec rursum quo pacto fugerit aestu.
in parvas igitur partis dispergitur umor
quas oculi nulla possunt ratione videre. 310
quin etiam multis solis redeuntibus annis
anulus in digito subter tenuatur habendo,
stilicidi casus lapidem cavat, uncus aratri
ferreus occulte decrescit vomer in arvis,
strataque iam volgi pedibus detrita viarum 315
saxea conspicimus; tum portas propter aena
signa manus dextras ostendunt attenuari
saepe salutantum tactu praeterque meantum.
haec igitur minui, cum sint detrita, videmus.
sed quae corpora decedant in tempore quoque 320
invida praeclusit speciem natura videndi.
postremo quaecumque dies naturaque rebus
paulatim tribuit, moderatim crescere cogens,

nulla potest oculorum acies contenta tueri,
nec porro quaecumque aevo macieque senescunt;   325
nec, mare quae impendent, vesco sale saxa peresa
quid quoque amittant in tempore cernere possis.
corporibus caecis igitur natura gerit res.

11 VOID (329-369)

Bodies aren't jammed in on every side:
there's Void in things.

you'll wish you'd known this
when you're staggering up the path of doubt
obsessively cross-examining the universe
because your faith in my words has lapsed.

take it from me
there's an empty place:
an untouched wilderness of Void.

if there was no Void, nothing could move
because it's the job of Body to get in the way:
Body is obstacle, sans exception.

Void is the space which lets things happen
without it nothing works
because there's no way for motion to begin.

but as it is, in earth, in sea, sky's gothic vaults
we see matter moving on myriad trajectories.

without Void
it's not so much that things would be deprived of motion
as that they would not exist at all
since matter wedged immobile
is incapable of forming shapes.

so, though things are solid to the eye
they're really just a scattering of atoms.

rocky grotto ceilings
let water through in fertile droplets

like milk dripping from teats.
food disperses through the bodies of living things.
orchards grow fruit according to season
because the whole tree sucks up food
from roots deep down
through trunk through branches
to the top.

voices coil catacombs and flit cloisters
seeping cold brings bones to a standstill
no way would you see these things happen
unless there was empty space
for Bodies to cross over.

why do you think one thing exceeds
something else in weight
although no bigger?
if there were as many Bodies
in a ball of wool as in a piece of lead
they'd weigh the same:
it's Body's job to weigh things down
it's Void's way to be weightless:
so what's big and light
declares itself as mainly Void;
what's small and heavy bears testimony
that it contains more Body
and less Void inside.

this mixture in matter is
the quarry we're sniffing out by intellect:
we call it Void.

nec tamen undique corporea stipata tenentur
omnia natura; namque est in rebus inane. 330
quod tibi cognosse in multis erit utile rebus
nec sinet errantem dubitare et quaerere semper
de summa rerum et nostris diffidere dictis.
quapropter locus est intactus inane vacansque.
quod si non esset, nulla ratione moveri 335
res possent; namque officium quod corporis exstat,
officere atque obstare, id in omni tempore adesset
omnibus; haud igitur quicquam procedere posset,
principium quoniam cedendi nulla daret res.
at nunc per maria ac terras sublimaque caeli 340
multa modis multis varia ratione moveri
cernimus ante oculos, quae, si non esset inane,
non tam sollicito motu privata carerent
quam genita omnino nulla ratione fuissent,
undique materies quoniam stipata quiesset. 345
praeterea quamvis solidae res esse putentur,
hinc tamen esse licet raro cum corpore cernas.
in saxis ac speluncis permanat aquarum
liquidus umor et uberibus flent omnia guttis.
dissipat in corpus sese cibus omne animantum. 350
crescunt arbusta et fetus in tempore fundunt,
quod cibus in totas usque ab radicibus imis
per truncos ac per ramos diffunditur omnis.
inter saepta meant voces et clausa domorum
transvolitant, rigidum permanat frigus ad ossa, 355
quod, nisi inania sint, qua possent corpora quaeque
transire, haud ulla fieri ratione videres.
denique cur alias aliis praestare videmus
pondere res rebus nihilo maiore figura?
nam si tantundemst in lanae glomere quantum 360
corporis in plumbo est, tantundem pendere par est,
corporis officiumst quoniam premere omnia deorsum,

contra autem natura manet sine pondere inanis.
ergo quod magnumst aeque leviusque videtur,
nimirum plus esse sibi declarat inanis;   365
at contra gravius plus in se corporis esse
dedicat et multo vacui minus intus habere.
est igitur nimirum id quod ratione sagaci
quaerimus, admixtum rebus, quod inane vocamus.

12 EXAMPLES OF VOID (370-397)

Now I'll launch an advance action
against those who make up theories
to seduce you from the truth.

some people say there is no Void.
the sea – they say – falls back
while phalanxes of fish in their advance
open up a highway with walls of water
like Moses in the Red Sea
because the fish leave space behind them
that the water can close up in.
they say this shows that things can move
although the world's packed full of matter.

this reasoning is blatant falsehood.

how would the chain-mailed phalanx make headway
if the water left no room for its procession?
where would the water go,
if the fish could not go forward?

you either have to say
that each stage in the process is deprived of motion
or that the universe is interfused with Void
which gives each thing the room to start to move.

when two extensive objects smack together
then bound apart – surely you can see
that air must seep into the gap between
and take possession of the Void.

but it isn't sucked straight in
in a great whoop of accelerating wind
it doesn't fill the whole space all at once

it colonizes spaces bit by bit
until it owns the whole.

whoever thinks our objects leapt apart
like a mechanism athwart a coiled spring of air
is wrong: if compressed air
moved in to fill the gap
then it would leave a Void around
which wasn't there before
at the same time as it filled a Void which was;
and anyhow –
air can't spontaneously thicken in this way
and even if it could
I don't think it could do it without Void –
fold in upon itself,
clasp all its limbs in one.

    illud in his rebus ne te deducere vero   370
    possit, quod quidam fingunt, praecurrere cogor.
    cedere squamigeris latices nitentibus aiunt
    et liquidas aperire vias, quia post loca pisces
    linquant, quo possint cedentes confluere undae.
    sic alias quoque res inter se posse moveri   375
    et mutare locum, quamvis sint omnia plena.
    scilicet id falsa totum ratione receptumst.
    nam quo squamigeri poterunt procedere tandem,
    ni spatium dederint latices? concedere porro
    quo poterunt undae, cum pisces ire nequibunt? 380
    aut igitur motu privandumst corpora quaeque
    aut esse admixtum dicendumst rebus inane
    unde initum primum capiat res quaeque movendi.
    postremo duo de concursu corpora lata
    si cita dissiliant, nempe aer omne necessest,   385

inter corpora quod fiat, possidat inane.
is porro quamvis circum celerantibus auris
confluat, haud poterit tamen uno tempore totum
compleri spatium; nam primum quemque necessest
occupet ille locum, deinde omnia possideantur. 390
quod si forte aliquis, cum corpora dissiluere,
tum putat id fieri quia se condenseat aer,
errat; nam vacuum tum fit quod non fuit ante
et repletur item vacuum quod constitit ante,
nec tali ratione potest denserier aer, 395
nec, si iam posset, sine inani posset, opinor,
ipse in se trahere et partis conducere in unum.

13 ENDLESS POSSIBILITIES FOR PROOF (398-417)

Interrogate the theory all you want:
you must admit there's Void in things.

I could ground the roots of my argument
as deeply as you like
pile proof on proof –
but your intellect will learn all by itself
to sniff out its quarry
with only a glance from me.

just like hounds crash mountain slopes
casting about for the boudoirs of beasts
behind leaf-screen and thicket
once they hit on a trail, they're off:
by following the line of scent I've laid
you too will penetrate every lair dark to sight
your jaws will close on truth and draw it out.

but if you slacken and pull back
I promise you this, my friend, for sure:
my fluent tongue can pour
a delta from the Mekong of my breast –
there's a such a landscape of verse in there
that I'm afraid time will release the locks
and let my life run out
before even one single rivulet
can pursue its course
over the wide meadowland of argument.

> quapropter, quamvis causando multa moreris,
> esse in rebus inane tamen fateare necessest.
> multaque praeterea tibi possum commemorando   400
> argumenta fidem dictis corradere nostris.

verum animo satis haec vestigia parva sagaci
sunt per quae possis cognoscere cetera tute.
namque canes ut montivagae persaepe ferarum
naribus inveniunt intectas fronde quietes, 405
cum semel institerunt vestigia certa viai,
sic alid ex alio per te tute ipse videre
talibus in rebus poteris caecasque latebras
insinuare omnis et verum protrahere inde.
quod si pigraris paulumve recesseris ab re, 410
hoc tibi de plano possum promittere, Memmi:
usque adeo largos haustus e fontibu' magnis
lingua meo suavis diti de pectore fundet,
ut verear ne tarda prius per membra senectus
serpat et in nobis vitai claustra resolvat, 415
quam tibi de quavis una re versibus omnis
argumentorum sit copia missa per auris.

14 VOID, CONTINUED (418-448)

Now – to rework the warp and weft of my words –
the whole of nature's two things only:
Body and Void.
Void is where Bodies are
and what they move around in.

the consensus of sensation
is the first and only evidence
that Body exists –
without our senses
we couldn't understand the world at all
the senses are the base-camp
whence our minds can start the climb
to hidden things.

so then this empty place – we call it Void –
without this there'd be nowhere
for Bodies to be, or move
about in on
their trajectories.

nature offers no third thing
discrete from all of Body, all of Void.

whatever exists is able to be touched –
however light your fingers'
butterfly-wing brush –
and if it can be touched
it stands as an addition
however large or small
to the totality of Matter.

but if something is intangible
if no part of it prevents an object
from passing through it on its path
then it's that negative space
we call Void.

the possibilities for movement are threefold:
Void and Body will themselves do something;
they will allow things to be done to them;
or they will provide the space
in which things act, or are performed.

to act or act upon can't happen without Body;
and the only thing that offers
a location for these acts
is empty space.

there's no third thing
left over by the sum of nature
no remainder which falls
outside the radar of our senses
nothing you can arrive at
by the mind's reach only.

> sed nunc ut repetam coeptum pertexere dictis,
> omnis, ut est igitur per se, natura duabus
> constitit in rebus; nam corpora sunt et inane,   420
> haec in quo sita sunt et qua diversa moventur.
> corpus enim per se communis dedicat esse
> sensus; cui nisi prima fides fundata valebit,
> haud erit occultis de rebus quo referentes
> confirmare animi quicquam ratione queamus.   425
> tum porro locus ac spatium, quod inane vocamus,

si nullum foret, haud usquam sita corpora possent
esse neque omnino quoquam diversa meare;
id quod iam supera tibi paulo ostendimus ante.
praeterea nil est quod possis dicere ab omni 430
corpore seiunctum secretumque esse ab inani,
quod quasi tertia sit numero natura reperta.
nam quodcumque erit, esse aliquid debebit id ipsum;
cui si tactus erit quamvis levis exiguusque, [435]
augmine vel grandi vel parvo denique, dum sit, 435 [434]
corporis augebit numerum summamque sequetur.
sin intactile erit, nulla de parte quod ullam
rem prohibere queat per se transire meantem,
scilicet hoc id erit, vacuum quod inane vocamus.
praeterea per se quodcumque erit, aut faciet quid 440
aut aliis fungi debebit agentibus ipsum
aut erit ut possint in eo res esse gerique.
at facere et fungi sine corpore nulla potest res
nec praebere locum porro nisi inane vacansque.
ergo praeter inane et corpora tertia per se 445
nulla potest rerum in numero natura relinqui,
nec quae sub sensus cadat ullo tempore nostros
nec ratione animi quam quisquam possit apisci.

15 TIME (449-482)

Everything that's got a name, you'll find
is either an assemblage
made out of Void and Body
or comes about because of them.

an assemblage is a marriage
between a thing and its properties
which can't be annulled
without the schism of disintegration
subdivision, separation from its
self – like weight from rocks
heat from fire, water from wet
Body's tangibility from
the evasiveness of Void.

very different are
slavery poverty wealth
freedom war consensus
and all those other things
whose comings and goings
we call events, but by which
the universe itself remains unmoved.

time has no existence of its own
outside our need for order –
what's done in time past
what begs our attention now
which result will follow
time is a human fabrication
it has no abstract life
apart from things in rest and things in motion.

history's an illusion
an accident of nature
whether on a global or a village scale:
world wars, genocide
the Scandals of the Old House –
be careful these don't take on
the lives of characters
in an historical drama
living in the here-and-now:
these events were products
of specific times, specific races
now (thank god) consigned to
death's oblivion.

history is a Trojan Horse of the mind:
it infiltrates walled cities
and fans the flames of war
by stealthy parturition of ideas.

we allow ourselves to be seduced
by history's illusion like a love-story:
it's kindled in our hearts no less
than a lover's face in an adulterer's breast.

we like to think there's more to life
than bodies moving round in space
but in reality
there is no possible reconstruction
of any momentary union of Void and Body
events we can base ideas on
such as justice, love or peace

just the chance coalescence of the past.

nam quaecumque cluent, aut his coniuncta duabus
rebus ea invenies aut horum eventa videbis.   450
coniunctum est id quod nusquam sine permitiali
discidio potis est seiungi seque gregari,
pondus uti saxis, calor ignist, liquor aquai,
tactus corporibus cunctis, intactus inani.
servitium contra paupertas divitiaeque,   455
libertas bellum concordia, cetera quorum
adventu manet incolumis natura abituque,
haec soliti sumus, ut par est, eventa vocare.
tempus item per se non est, sed rebus ab ipsis
consequitur sensus, transactum quid sit in aevo, 460
tum quae res instet, quid porro deinde sequatur.
nec per se quemquam tempus sentire fatendumst
semotum ab rerum motu placidaque quiete.
denique Tyndaridem raptam belloque subactas
Troiugenas gentis cum dicunt esse, videndumst   465
ne forte haec per se cogant nos esse fateri,
quando ea saecla hominum, quorum haec eventa fuerunt,
inrevocabilis abstulerit iam praeterita aetas.
namque aliud terris, aliud regionibus ipsis
eventum dici poterit quodcumque erit actum.   470
denique materies si rerum nulla fuisset
nec locus ac spatium, res in quo quaeque geruntur,
numquam Tyndaridis forma conflatus amoris
ignis, Alexandri Phrygio sub pectore gliscens,
clara accendisset saevi certamina belli,   475
nec clam durateus Troianis Pergama partu
inflammasset equus nocturno Graiugenarum;
perspicere ut possis res gestas funditus omnis
non ita uti corpus per se constare neque esse,
nec ratione cluere eadem qua constet inane,   480
sed magis ut merito possis eventa vocare
corporis atque loci, res in quo quaeque gerantur.

16 MATTER IS SOLID, SEPARATE, ETERNAL (483-598)

Entities are made
partly of unmixed atoms
partly of self-sustaining combinations.
their smallest parts cannot be quenched:
they stand solid in the face of time.

all the same, it's difficult to grasp
that there's anything so solid.

a thunderclap from heaven
coils corridors like someone calling;
iron steals fire's candescence from the flames
hot rocks crack open with a noxious whiff;
a solid mass of gold becomes a river
bronze ice melts in a metal-worker's furnace

heat and thrusting cold track right through silver
we know this when we lift the ritual chalice
and feel the metal, warm as living flesh just now,
grow cold with condensation
when the libation's poured
in from above.

it seems there's no solidity in things.

but let me carry you along a little
while I explain in an economy of verse
that the universe's fundamental core
stands firm and indestructible –
I mean, the lowest you can go, the Primary Parts
from which all we see is put together.

since we've established that
the world is made of two things –

two things only –
that all its vast diversity
can be accounted for
by interplay of Body and of Space –
Space being where every last event takes place –
know furthermore that each of these
must be discrete and uninflected by the other.
for Space – what we call Void –
is bodiless by nature; where
soever Body puts itself
this can by definition not be Void.

so we see the building blocks of matter must be solid
and completely free of Void.

but since there's space in all things, once created,
Void must lie in matter's warm embrace;
nothing could wrap the Void around
encompass and protect it
like a womb an embryo
unless something solid was left out
to do the wrapping round:
matter's circumfluescence
confines the Void in things.

then, too, since matter stands
endowed with solid Body
it has to be eternal, and survive
the dissolution of its passing shapes.

if no space offered its neutrality
the world would jostle jam-packed
like a football crowd;
and if there were no bodies

cut to size to fill their space
the universe would be an empty stadium.

Body and Void take turns –
Full and Empty don't win outright.

bodies with fixed limits
interspersed in space
bring colour to its blank ubiety.
these bodies are the universe's base
they don't dissolve to nothing
even when bombarded from outside;
and their fabric won't unravel
however deep destruction's moth
might burrow in.

in fact, you can't destroy them any way at all:
by demolition or dissection
by grinding them like spices in a mortar
you only squeeze out intervening Void
they can't take on water
or be split like rocks when frost gets in
or be consumed by fire
which makes an end of all created things.

the more Void a compound contains
the more deeply it can be harmed in all these ways –
but when solid and without Void
nature's smallest parts must be eternal.

if matter weren't eternal
everything we see would be reduced to nothing
long ago, and have to be rebuilt ground up.

but since I've taught things can't be made from nothing,
and no single thing, once made, revoked to nothingness –
matter's smallest parts must then possess
imperishable being; so when the time is ripe
released from their contracted roles
they become again the raw material
of a universe in constant reconstruction.

First Bodies must be solid simple things –
else how are they preserved till now,
across a time so vast its reckoning-point is lost?

then too, if Nature hadn't made the rule
that things can't be broken up beyond a certain point,
time's infinitely iterated blows would
long since have pulverized matter to a size
so small that nothing could be built from it
big enough to survive.

for obviously any thing you like
can be destroyed more quickly than replaced;
because of this, all things
which the long ongoing span
of time outlived before has disassembled,
stripping them down and throwing away the parts,
could never be repaired
no matter how much time remained.

but there's a limit to disaggregation
a line which can't be crossed
we know because we see each thing replenished
its growth's parameters fixed according to species
until the finished being comes to flower.

because of the solidity of bodies
nature can render any grade of alloy
from its raw materials, from soft to hard
according to how much Void is in the mix.
so we get air, water, earth, and flames of fire.

if those First Bodies were soft in any way
where would you get resilient rocks
and iron? – there's no way these could happen
if their nature had no fundament to start from.

their state as simple solids is what gives
the Primary Particles their power:
they can be forced together under pressure
piled up like a pyramid of body-builders
in a collective architecture that is super-strong.

but even if there was no limit
to the breaking-up of bodies
nonetheless far back as you can see
some constituents must stay intact
never yet threatened with oblivion.

it doesn't square with reality to imagine
that anything that can go on breaking up
could have survived the relentless blows
of time's interrogation.

a proper limit has been placed on things
whose growth and fragile tenancy of light
is terminated according to species;
which freedoms nature's contract has allowed them,
which it has curtailed
at the drawing-up of the Document of Life

a statute that can never be repealed
but is inscribed in stone
down to the final detail.

change is the surface gloss of constancy:
so the technicolour plumages of birds
conceal the fact that underneath the wings
they're just airborne clusters
of the same unchanging matter.

for if the document of nature was annulled
its rules rewritten in another language
then we would be uncertain
what forms things can take
what's impossible
why the limitations
where the boundary-stone of the cosmos
lies, its foot sunk deep –

without some genoglu blueprint
- the progeny would not repeat
their parents' phenotype –
how each looks, moves, and eats.

        corpora sunt porro partim primordia rerum,
        partim concilio quae constant principiorum.
        sed quae sunt rerum primordia, nulla potest vis 485
        stinguere; nam solido vincunt ea corpore demum.
        etsi difficile esse videtur credere quicquam
        in rebus solido reperiri corpore posse.
        transit enim fulmen caeli per saepta domorum,
        clamor ut ac voces; ferrum candescit in igni   490
        dissiliuntque fero ferventi saxa vapore;

tum labefactatus rigor auri solvitur aestu;
tum glacies aeris flamma devicta liquescit;
permanat calor argentum penetraleque frigus,
quando utrumque manu retinentes pocula rite 495
sensimus infuso lympharum rore superne.
usque adeo in rebus solidi nihil esse videtur.
sed quia vera tamen ratio naturaque rerum
cogit, ades, paucis dum versibus expediamus
esse ea quae solido atque aeterno corpore constent, 500
semina quae rerum primordiaque esse docemus,
unde omnis rerum nunc constet summa creata.
Principio quoniam duplex natura duarum
dissimilis rerum longe constare repertast,
corporis atque loci, res in quo quaeque geruntur, 505
esse utramque sibi per se puramque necessest.
nam quacumque vacat spatium, quod inane vocamus,
corpus ea non est; qua porro cumque tenet se
corpus, ea vacuum nequaquam constat inane.
sunt igitur solida ac sine inani corpora prima. 510
praeterea quoniam genitis in rebus inanest,
materiem circum solidam constare necessest,
nec res ulla potest vera ratione probari
corpore inane suo celare atque intus habere,
si non, quod cohibet, solidum constare relinquas. 515
id porro nihil esse potest nisi materiai
concilium, quod inane queat rerum cohibere.
materies igitur, solido quae corpore constat,
esse aeterna potest, cum cetera dissoluantur.
tum porro si nil esset quod inane vocaret, 520
omne foret solidum; nisi contra corpora certa
essent quae loca complerent quaecumque tenerent,
omne quod est spatium vacuum constaret inane.
alternis igitur nimirum corpus inani
distinctumst, quoniam nec plenum naviter exstat 525

nec porro vacuum. sunt ergo corpora certa
quae spatium pleno possint distinguere inane.
haec neque dissolui plagis extrinsecus icta
possunt nec porro penitus penetrata retexi
nec ratione queunt alia temptata labare; 530
id quod iam supra tibi paulo ostendimus ante.
nam neque collidi sine inani posse videtur
quicquam nec frangi nec findi in bina secando
nec capere umorem neque item manabile frigus
nec penetralem ignem, quibus omnia conficiuntur. 535
et quo quaeque magis cohibet res intus inane,
tam magis his rebus penitus temptata labascit.
ergo si solida ac sine inani corpora prima
sunt ita uti docui, sint haec aeterna necessest.
praeterea nisi materies aeterna fuisset, 540
antehac ad nilum penitus res quaeque redissent
de niloque renata forent quae cumque videmus.
at quoniam supra docui nil posse creari
de nilo neque quod genitum est ad nil revocari,
esse immortali primordia corpore debent, 545
dissolui quo quaeque supremo tempore possint,
materies ut suppeditet rebus reparandis.
sunt igitur solida primordia simplicitate
nec ratione queunt alia servata per aevum
ex infinito iam tempore res reparare. 550
Denique si nullam finem natura parasset
frangendis rebus, iam corpora materiai
usque redacta forent aevo frangente priore,
ut nil ex illis a certo tempore posset
conceptum <ad> summum aetatis pervadere finem. 555
nam quidvis citius dissolvi posse videmus
quam rursus refici; quapropter longa diei
infinita aetas anteacti temporis omnis
quod fregisset adhuc disturbans dissoluensque,

numquam reliquo reparari tempore posset. 560
at nunc nimirum frangendi reddita finis
certa manet, quoniam refici rem quamque videmus
et finita simul generatim tempora rebus
stare, quibus possint aevi contingere florem.
huc accedit uti, solidissima materiai 565
corpora cum constant, possint tamen omnia reddi,
mollia quae fiunt, aer aqua terra vapores,
quo pacto fiant et qua vi quaeque gerantur,
admixtum quoniam semel est in rebus inane.
at contra si mollia sint primordia rerum, 570
unde queant validi silices ferrumque creari
non poterit ratio reddi; nam funditus omnis
principio fundamenti natura carebit.
sunt igitur solida pollentia simplicitate
quorum condenso magis omnia conciliatu 575
artari possunt validasque ostendere viris.
porro si nullast frangendis reddita finis
corporibus, tamen ex aeterno tempore quaeque
nunc etiam superare necessest corpora rebus,
quae nondum clueant ullo temptata periclo. 580
at quoniam fragili natura praedita constant,
discrepat aeternum tempus potuisse manere
innumerabilibus plagis vexata per aevum.
Denique iam quoniam generatim reddita finis
crescendi rebus constat vitamque tenendi, 585
et quid quaeque queant per foedera naturai,
quid porro nequeant, sancitum quandoquidem exstat,
nec commutatur quicquam, quin omnia constant
usque adeo, variae volucres ut in ordine cunctae
ostendant maculas generalis corpore inesse, 590
immutabili' materiae quoque corpus habere
debent nimirum. nam si primordia rerum
commutari aliqua possent ratione revicta,

incertum quoque iam constet quid possit oriri,
quid nequeat, finita potestas denique cuique   595
quanam sit ratione atque alte terminus haerens,
nec totiens possent generatim saecla referre
naturam mores victum motusque parentum.

17 ATOMS CAN'T BE CUT (599-634)

Since, then, the smallest point of matter
lies beneath the radar of our senses
each tiny part must be without parts itself
unable to exist at all outside of what it's part of.

this is how our pyramid of matter
stacks up, part on part in order
like a cheerleading team on display
and because its parts cannot exist alone
they must have a way to stick together
so they can't fall out from the formation.

these particles are solid simple things
lots of tiny bodies packed together
their source of power not so much
mutual consensus as single-minded endurance.
they can't be picked apart or shrunk
nature needs to hold them in reserve as
the raw materials for rebuilding of the whole.

without a limit to the breaking-up of bodies
nature's hall of mirrors would recede forever
everything an image of itself –
and then what difference will there be
between the universe's totality
and its tiny parts?
none at all – for as the universe itself
is altogether limitless, so too
its smallest components would be
limitless in their divisibility,
infinitely tiny worlds within a world.

since the voice of reason decries the idea
that the biggest and the smallest things

could be the same
you must admit defeat
and say that there are things
whose job it is to be the smallest, without parts,
solid and eternal.

if nature, creator of the universe
was in the habit of forcing everything
into smaller and smaller parts,
not even she could rebuild anything then;
only when nature's fusion chamber
is filled with tiny parts
that cannot be themselves divided
and these are galvanized by fruitful motion –
concursions impacts compressions violent thrustings –
can she give birth to every kind of matter.

> tum porro quoniam est extremum quodque cacumen
> *
> corporis illius, quod nostri cernere sensus   600
> iam nequeunt, id nimirum sine partibus extat
> et minima constat natura nec fuit umquam
> per se secretum neque posthac esse valebit,
> alterius quoniamst ipsum pars, primaque et una,
> inde aliae atque aliae similes ex ordine partes   605
> agmine condenso naturam corporis explent,
> quae quoniam per se nequeunt constare, necessest
> haerere unde queant nulla ratione revelli.
> sunt igitur solida primordia simplicitate
> quae minimis stipata cohaerent partibus arte,   610
> non ex illarum conventu conciliata,
> sed magis aeterna pollentia simplicitate,

unde neque avelli quicquam neque deminui iam
concedit natura reservans semina rebus.
praeterea nisi erit minimum, parvissima quaeque   615
corpora constabunt ex partibus infinitis,
quippe ubi dimidiae partis pars semper habebit
dimidiam partem nec res praefiniet ulla.
ergo rerum inter summam minimamque quod escit?
nil erit ut distet; nam quamvis funditus omnis   620
summa sit infinita, tamen, parvissima quae sunt,
ex infinitis constabunt partibus aeque.
quod quoniam ratio reclamat vera negatque
credere posse animum, victus fateare necessest
esse ea quae nullis iam praedita partibus exstent   625
et minima constent natura. quae quoniam sunt,
illa quoque esse tibi solida atque aeterna fatendum.
denique si minimas in partis cuncta resolvi
cogere consuesset rerum natura creatrix,
iam nil ex illis eadem reparare valeret   630
propterea quia, quae nullis sunt partibus aucta,
non possunt ea quae debet genitalis habere
materies, varios conexus pondera plagas
concursus motus, per quas res quaeque geruntur.

18 DELUDED THEORIES 1: HERACLITUS (635-711)

There was a time when people said
the universe was made of fire – and only fire –
although we think them seriously deluded.

Heraclitus was the leader of this pack –
his ostentatious obscurity made him famous
with airheads who think that jargon
is worth money, rather than with
simple seekers after truths.

stupid people are convinced by what they find
lurking in twisted thickets
and think things must be true
if only they ring in the ears,
deep dyed with rainbow sounds.

for why are there so many different things,
I want to know, if they are made
of unadulterated fire alone?
what would be the use
of diluting or condensing fire
if fire's constituents all share the makeup
of fire writ large?

fire's nature's to be hot or hotter:
more concentrated fire would sear more fiercely;
a gentle warmth would come from rare-
faction.

this is all you can expect from fire
not infinite variety of things.

if these True Believers would admit
there must be Void in everything

that fire could be compacted
or thinly scattered
according to how much Void you add –
then at least their argument would boil down
to two things – fire and Void

but because their oracular musings mutter
about all sorts of contrary-to-facts
they won't admit that Void exists
they run off-piste whilst looking for the easy route
they fail to see that once you sunder Void from things
there's nothing left but one big mass of matter
which can't itself give anything away, instead
sucks the whole lot in like a black hole –
but generous fire pours out light and heat
as unalleviated matter just can't do.

if they believe that fire
by taking on some crystal structure
stops burning and changes form –
sure, if it does this without stint
then every shred of its identity will perish.

for whatever exceeds the decree of its existence
is death to what it was before.

so for their argument to work
something must be left intact
or – there you go! – the universe would vanish
and the whole diversity of nature
have to be rebuilt from the ground up.

but there are stable bodies
which retain their selfhood for eternity

they come and go
their place exchanged, the nature's changed
of whatever they create
in their never-ending relay
they take on form as fire could never do.

if particles of fire retain fire's being
let them fall out, vanish
be assigned to something else
change places in the lineup –
look at it any way you like –
what they make is always fire.

the truth is this, I think:
there are basic bodies whose
covent motion position order structure
make fire – or anything –
and by changing places, change the nature
of whatever they create; but they themselves
are not like fire – not like anything, in fact
which stumbles by its reach upon our touch.

to say that everything is fire – and more –
to say that nothing exists at all
which is not fire
is total madness.

think what it would be like
if everything was fire.
it's contrary to the data of our senses.
our senses are the only interface
between our selves and the world.
we have to trust them
as the only way into what we believe.

if we are forced to state
what doesn't chime
with what our senses tell us,
then they – and we – will crumble.
our senses are how we know that fire is fire.
through them we recognize true fire
and reject the rest
though no less bright.

it's empty raving to deny the senses credence.
we have no certainty, no means of separation
of truth from lies
other than by our senses.

where's that leave us, then?
is it any better to strip away
everything else and just leave fire as real
or to say that fire is something other than it seems?
– either way lies madness.

so those who think that fire
is the universe's underlying stuff
like those who think
that air's the building-block of things
those who rely
on the constructive power of water
or say that earth's chameleon nature
can take on any form it pleases – they all
took a wrong turning on the road to truth
a long long time ago.

we think that we've moved on, evolved:
that modernity gives less scope
for blind belief – yet still

the Theory of Everything
the God-particle, the One True Answer
draw us in.

Science offers us no One Solution,
though useful for what it says
about what's human: the need
to wish for one.

    quapropter qui materiem rerum esse putarunt   635
    ignem atque ex igni summam consistere solo,
    magno opere a vera lapsi ratione videntur.
    Heraclitus init quorum dux proelia primus,
    clarus <ob> obscuram linguam magis inter inanis
    quamde gravis inter Graios qui vera requirunt.   640
    omnia enim stolidi magis admirantur amantque,
    inversis quae sub verbis latitantia cernunt,
    veraque constituunt quae belle tangere possunt
    auris et lepido quae sunt fucata sonore.
    nam cur tam variae res possent esse requiro,   645
    ex uno si sunt igni puroque creatae.
    nil prodesset enim calidum denserier ignem
    nec rarefieri, si partes ignis eandem
    naturam quam totus habet super ignis haberent.
    acrior ardor enim conductis partibus esset,   650
    languidior porro disiectis disque sipatis.
    amplius hoc fieri nihil est quod posse rearis
    talibus in causis, nedum variantia rerum
    tanta queat densis rarisque ex ignibus esse.
    id quoque, si faciant admixtum rebus inane,   655
    denseri poterunt ignes rarique relinqui.
    sed quia multa sibi cernunt contraria †muset†
    et fugitant in rebus inane relinquere purum,

ardua dum metuunt, amittunt vera viai,
nec rursum cernunt exempto rebus inani 660
omnia denseri fierique ex omnibus unum
corpus, nil ab se quod possit mittere raptim;
aestifer ignis uti lumen iacit atque vaporem,
ut videas non e stipatis partibus esse.
quod si forte alia credunt ratione potesse 665
ignis in coetu stingui mutareque corpus,
scilicet ex nulla facere id si parte reparcent,
occidet ad nilum nimirum funditus ardor
omnis et <e> nilo fient quae cumque creantur.
nam quodcumque suis mutatum finibus exit, 670
continuo hoc mors est illius quod fuit ante.
proinde aliquid superare necesse est incolume ollis,
ne tibi res redeant ad nilum funditus omnes
de niloque renata vigescat copia rerum.
nunc igitur quoniam certissima corpora quaedam 675
sunt quae conservant naturam semper eandem,
quorum abitu aut aditu mutatoque ordine mutant
naturam res et convertunt corpora sese,
scire licet non esse haec ignea corpora rerum.
nil referret enim quaedam decedere, abire, 680
atque alia attribui, mutarique ordine quaedam,
si tamen ardoris naturam cuncta tenerent;
ignis enim foret omnimodis quodcumque crearent.
verum, ut opinor, itast: sunt quaedam corpora quorum
concursus motus ordo positura figurae 685
efficiunt ignis, mutatoque ordine mutant
naturam neque sunt igni simulata neque ulli
praeterea rei quae corpora mittere possit
sensibus et nostros adiectu tangere tactus.
Dicere porro ignem res omnis esse neque ullam 690
rem veram in numero rerum constare nisi ignem,
quod facit hic idem, perdelirum esse videtur.

nam contra sensus ab sensibus ipse repugnat
et labefactat eos, unde omnia credita pendent,
unde hic cognitus est ipsi quem nominat ignem.   695
credit enim sensus ignem cognoscere vere,
cetera non credit, quae nilo clara minus sunt.
quod mihi cum vanum tum delirum esse videtur.
quo referemus enim? quid nobis certius ipsis
sensibus esse potest, qui vera ac falsa notemus?   700
praeterea quare quisquam magis omnia tollat
et velit ardoris naturam linquere solam,
quam neget esse ignis, <aliam> tamen esse relinquat?
aequa videtur enim dementia dicere utrumque.
Quapropter qui materiem rerum esse putarunt   705
ignem atque ex igni summam consistere posse,
et qui principium gignundis aera rebus
constituere, aut umorem qui cumque putarunt
fingere res ipsum per se, terramve creare
omnia et in rerum naturas vertier omnis,   710
magno opere a vero longe derrasse videntur.

19 DELUDED THEORIES 2: EMPEDOCLES (712-829)

Then there are those
who make a Noah's Ark of elements
a two-by-two procession
of air and fire, water and earth
and say these four –
fire earth breath rain –
between them make the universe.

among these is Empedocles
born on his three-cornered hat of an island
whose coast the breakers of the Ionian sea
paint with verdigris
and a narrow greedy strait divides
from the Italian shore.

on one side the blowhole yapping
lapping like a mad dog with its tongue of foam;
on the other Etna threatening
through its flames' still muffled crack and snap
that its powerful jaws will once again disgorge
a jet of fire tall enough
to strike the vaulted ceiling of the sky.

you have to see this place:
it counts its marvels cheap
crammed with produce
well stocked with muniments of men
but there's nothing more amazing
more worthy of wonder and worship
than Empedocles.

it's true – he transcends the human race;
the poems that burst from his breast

and flame his glowing thoughts
might be the utterances of a god.

his mountain-top intelligence stands out
from the throng of those whose eminence
is far behind in scale – but even so
he's just as wrong as all those other elementalists
though their near-divine discoveries
are like oracles delivered from the heart's shrine
and much more true than those
the priestess prophetess pours forth
from Apollo's laurelled tripod-seat.

but they all come crashing down
along with the furniture of a universe
whose foundations they've undermined –
first of all because they allow motion
whilst subtracting Void –
they say that things are soft and seethrough
air fire light
crops and living things
but they don't allow Void
to mitigate the mass in them;
second because they don't put any limit
on the fracturing of bodies
or stop the endless march of subdivision.

but, as we've seen, what lies beneath
the radar of our senses
constitutes the minimum:
the smallest thing is what we find
when we pass through the doors
between perception and conjecture:
the vanishing point beyond which vision fails.

because they are resolved to think
the things they call the fundamental particles –
these compounds which we say are born
endowed deep-down with finite span of life –
can take on different powers:
if this is so, the universe rewinds to zero
the whole diversity of nature
has to be rebuilt from the ground up;
we've seen that this can't happen.

then again, their elements are poised
in comprehensive enmity with one another
their coexistence mutual poison:
they meet – they die
exploding outwards in some chemical cascade
like new-year pyrotechnics –
strontium red
barium green
copper blue
white like magnesium –
quenching themselves in fall.

what's more, if their whole cycle of creation
arises from four elements, and returns to these
which comes first? elements from things, or the reverse?
these elements (we're told) unceasingly
assume each other's essence
pass through their colour spectrum
shed their former nature like a snake its skin.

but if you think that fire can mate with earth
and earth with breath of air and bead of dew
and yet remain themselves, although in congress –

no single thing arises from this marriage:
nothing souled, and nothing soulless (like a tree).

everything in this multicoloured heap
retains its very nature: their world's
a variegated pile of beads where
air with earth and fire with moisture
are jumbled up, but each one true to type.

no – in the process of creation
First Bodies must be self-effacing
hidden, achromatic, dark to sight:
a particle with a personality too strong
will hinder and obstruct whatever's made
from taking up the call to be itself.

these people take their cue from heaven and its fires
and first make fire transform itself to air
and air give birth to rain, and rain to earth
then – reversing in an upward train –
earth to rain and rain to air and air to fire
unceasing transmutation transmigration
dancing the elemental shuffle
from heaven down to earth
and back again from earth to stars of heaven.

there's no way Primary Parts behave like this.

there must be something left which doesn't change
or the data of the universe is wiped.
for whatever exceeds the decree of its existence
is death to what it was before.

elements with fugitive identity
must necessarily be made of smaller parts,
parts which aren't susceptible to change
or – there you go! – the world would vanish yet again.

our particles, gifted with adaptability
one moment come together to make fire;
but take away or add a few
change their position
their speed of oscillation
and you have a puff of air:
so things run through the open mesh of nature
cohering now and then in passing forms.

'But' you'll say 'my eyes don't lie:
upward-tending growth from earth to air
is real – crops plantations stock
would never grow unless, when time is ripe,
the seasons humour them with showers
groves shake, stripped by storms
sun in its turn takes care of them.'

you're right: in our case too,
lacking solid food or lucid water,
the body's wasting wrings the life
from every bone and muscle.

there's no doubt specific things
nourish us, while different lives
need different springs of growth
not because they're made of elements, but because
their particles are property held in common:
in the diagram of life, many particles
lie in an intersecting field

common to many living things.
everything's made up of Primary Parts
mixed in different proportions
so different lives need different fonts of growth.

though particles are common property,
it makes all the difference
what they lie next to
in what configuration they are placed
how they knock against each other
in this game of micro-snooker:
this is what clinches identity.

the same stuff makes up earth
sea sky sun rivers
crops plantations stock
but in each the particles
line up in different figures on the baize.

or think of particles as letters
like the ones you're reading now:
those that serve to make the verse
can also change the verse to serve
a different sound and meaning
if you just shuffle their positions.

if the letters of the Roman alphabet
can conjure up new words
just by changing order
how much more do you suppose
the primary particles – graphemes
in a cosmic game of scrabble –
create new worlds
limitless in combination?

adde etiam qui conduplicant primordia rerum
aera iungentes igni terramque liquori,
et qui quattuor ex rebus posse omnia rentur
ex igni terra atque anima procrescere et imbri. 715
quorum Acragantinus cum primis Empedocles est,
insula quem triquetris terrarum gessit in oris,
quam fluitans circum magnis anfractibus aequor
Ionium glaucis aspergit virus ab undis,
angustoque fretu rapidum mare dividit undis 720
Italiae terrarum oras a finibus eius.
hic est vasta Charybdis et hic Aetnaea minantur
murmura flammarum rursum se colligere iras,
faucibus eruptos iterum vis ut vomat ignis
ad caelumque ferat flammai fulgura rursum. 725
quae cum magna modis multis miranda videtur
gentibus humanis regio visendaque fertur,
rebus opima bonis, multa munita virum vi,
nil tamen hoc habuisse viro praeclarius in se
nec sanctum magis et mirum carumque videtur. 730
carmina quin etiam divini pectoris eius
vociferantur et exponunt praeclara reperta,
ut vix humana videatur stirpe creatus.
Hic tamen et supra quos diximus inferiores
partibus egregie multis multoque minores, 735
quamquam multa bene ac divinitus invenientes
ex adyto tamquam cordis responsa dedere
sanctius et multo certa ratione magis quam
Pythia quae tripodi a Phoebi lauroque profatur,
principiis tamen in rerum fecere ruinas 740
et graviter magni magno cecidere ibi casu;
primum quod motus exempto rebus inani
constituunt et res mollis rarasque relinquunt,
aera solem ignem terras animalia fruges,
nec tamen admiscent in eorum corpus inane; 745

deinde quod omnino finem non esse secandis
corporibus faciunt neque pausam stare fragori
nec prorsum in rebus minimum consistere quicquam;
cum videamus id extremum cuiusque cacumen
esse quod ad sensus nostros minimum esse videtur, 750
conicere ut possis ex hoc, quae cernere non quis
extremum quod habent, minimum consistere <in illis>.
huc accedit item, quoniam primordia rerum
mollia constituunt, quae nos nativa videmus
esse et mortali cum corpore funditus, utqui 755
debeat ad nilum iam rerum summa reverti
de niloque renata vigescere copia rerum;
quorum utrumque quid a vero iam distet habebis.
deinde inimica modis multis sunt atque veneno
ipsa sibi inter se; quare aut congressa peribunt 760
aut ita diffugient ut tempestate coacta
fulmina diffugere atque imbris ventosque videmus.
Denique quattuor ex rebus si cuncta creantur
atque in eas rursus res omnia dissoluuntur,
qui magis illa queunt rerum primordia dici 765
quam contra res illorum retroque putari?
alternis gignuntur enim mutantque colorem
et totam inter se naturam tempore ab omni.
sin ita forte putas ignis terraeque coire 770
corpus et aerias auras roremque liquoris,
nil in concilio naturam ut mutet eorum,
nulla tibi ex illis poterit res esse creata,
non animans, non exanimo cum corpore, ut arbor.
quippe suam quidque in coetu variantis acervi 775
naturam ostendet mixtusque videbitur aer
cum terra simul et quodam cum rore manere.
at primordia gignundis in rebus oportet
naturam clandestinam caecamque adhibere,
emineat nequid quod contra pugnet et obstet 780

quominus esse queat proprie quodcumque creatur.
Quin etiam repetunt a caelo atque ignibus eius
et primum faciunt ignem se vertere in auras
aeris, hinc imbrem gigni terramque creari
ex imbri retroque a terra cuncta reverti, 785
umorem primum, post aera, deinde calorem,
nec cessare haec inter se mutare, meare
a caelo ad terram, de terra ad sidera mundi.
quod facere haud ullo debent primordia pacto.
immutabile enim quiddam superare necessest, 790
ne res ad nihilum redigantur funditus omnes.
nam quodcumque suis mutatum finibus exit,
continuo hoc mors est illius quod fuit ante.
quapropter quoniam quae paulo diximus ante
in commutatum veniunt, constare necessest 795
ex aliis ea, quae nequeant convertier usquam,
ne tibi res redeant ad nilum funditus omnis.
quin potius tali natura praedita quaedam
corpora constituas, ignem si forte crearint,
posse eadem demptis paucis paucisque tributis, 800
ordine mutato et motu, facere aeris auras,
sic alias aliis rebus mutarier omnis?
'at manifesta palam res indicat' inquis 'in auras
aeris e terra res omnis crescere alique;
et nisi tempestas indulget tempore fausto 805
imbribus, ut tabe nimborum arbusta vacillent,
solque sua pro parte fovet tribuitque calorem,
crescere non possint fruges arbusta animantis.'
scilicet et nisi nos cibus aridus et tener umor
adiuvet, amisso iam corpore vita quoque omnis 810
omnibus e nervis atque ossibus exsoluatur.
adiutamur enim dubio procul atque alimur nos
certis ab rebus, certis aliae atque aliae res.
nimirum quia multa modis communia multis

multarum rerum in rebus primordia mixta 815
sunt, ideo variis variae res rebus aluntur.
atque eadem magni refert primordia saepe
cum quibus et quali positura contineantur
et quos inter se dent motus accipiantque;
namque eadem caelum mare terras flumina solem 820
constituunt, eadem fruges arbusta animantis,
verum aliis alioque modo commixta moventur.
quin etiam passim nostris in versibus ipsis
multa elementa vides multis communia verbis,
cum tamen inter se versus ac verba necessest 825
confiteare et re et sonitu distare sonanti.
tantum elementa queunt permutato ordine solo.
at rerum quae sunt primordia, plura adhibere
possunt unde queant variae res quaeque creari.

20 DELUDED THEORIES 3: ANAXAGORAS (830-920)

Now let's take a look
at Anaxagoras' homoeomeria.
whose what?
Lucretius couldn't do it in Latin
I can't in English;
only Greek – or German –
comes up with words like this.

its meaning (more or less) is 'like-in-limb'
the concept's easy
though intractable in words.
it means self-similarity,
Teilähnlichkeit, 'part-likeness'
where everything's a fractal of itself –
bones under the microscope
turn out to be made of tiny bones
guts of even tinier guts
blood of minuscule but mutually
cohesive nano-drips of blood;
gold is made of tiny flakes of gold
earth from mini-earths
fire from fairy fires
water from subscale water drops.

Anaxagoras makes out – perhaps believes –
that everything's constructed in this way.
this same man will not admit
Void into his *Wissenschaft*
or put an end to subdivision.
in both respects he's just as wrong
as those we've seen before.

and then, he makes his particles too weak:
his Primary Parts can be subjected just the same

to forces which erode the things they make;
their death becomes the road
to universal self-destruction.

which one of them has resilience
to evade annihilation under pressure,
to wrench itself away last-minute
from the snapping teeth of death?
fire water air? which one of these?
blood and bones? none I think:
for every part of them
would perish equally, right down to the roots.

but the universe cannot rewind to nothing
or grow back from nothing, as I've proved before.

we know that food
nourishes the whole body,
veins and blood and bones:
this being so, our guru must pretend
that food has whole anatomies mixed in
bodies with all their component parts –
tendon strings and bones and veins and blood –
so all food, wet and dry
is made of things which differ from itself –
what looks like food, in fact would have to be
a soup of bones and tendons
white cells red cells all combined in
an alphabet spaghetti of dismembered parts.

then again, whatever grows from earth
if contained in earth, would serve to prove
that earth must be composed of parts
divergent from itself, that rise from it.

whichever way you spin, the argument's the same.

if flame and smoke and ash skulk hid in wood
then wood is made of things divergent from itself.
earth makes trees, and trees make wood –
and wood makes smoke and ash and flame –
and all these things are different from eachother.

there's a scant amount of cover left
for Anaxagoras to hide behind
but he makes the most of it:
he thinks that all things sneakily conceal
a little bit of everything inside
but we only see what's present at the front.

this is a long way from the truth.

if so, grains of wheat would bleed
like limbs crushed by the millstone –
the mortar would show forensic traces
of blood or other substances the body produces

by the same token, you'd think grass and water
would yield drops with the same sweet taste
as milk which drips from teats of woolly ewes;
clods of earth, broken under the hoe, would be
sprinked with minute sprigs of leaf
ears of corn, different types of grasses
logs split with the axe should offer up
the germ of ash and smoke
if tiny fires lie hid inside.

since none of these things happen
the entities we see are not composed

of tiny ears of corn and sparks of fire
drops of serum, blood, milk, grains of earth.

what does lie hidden
is a multipurpose package,
a reservoir of primary particles
mingled among things.

'But we've all seen wildfires start in forests
in high winds, when the friction of their mutual embrace
decks the trees with sudden flowers
of tinsel flame.'

so you say – but trees spontaneously combust
not because their timber harbours embers,
but when many particles of heat
crowd in around the points of friction
and conspire to set the woods ablaze.

if flame lurks in the undergrowth
these fires must out:
so you'd see woods smoulder all the time
and forests razed to ash.

don't you see
it makes a massive difference
what particles lie next to
in what configuration they are placed
the way they knock against each other
and how, with just a minor switch
those same particles can make
timber into ember
just like the words themselves?

to loose the tie which binds
the letters to their words
to substitute some others in their place
makes vocables of different sound and sense:
a little change within in a word
conjures in the mind a world
near-infinite in colour, flavour
texture, scent and sound.

if you think the structure of the universe
can only be accounted for
by top to toe self-similarity:
imagine! it's like the particles themselves
would burst out laughing
the universe around them shake
and quake with mirth,
salt tears pour down its cheeks.

    nunc et Anaxagorae scrutemur homoeomerian   830
    quam Grai memorant nec nostra dicere lingua
    concedit nobis patrii sermonis egestas,
    sed tamen ipsam rem facilest exponere verbis.
    principio, rerum quam dicit homoeomerian,
    ossa videlicet e pauxillis atque minutis   835
    ossibus hic et de pauxillis atque minutis
    visceribus viscus gigni sanguenque creari
    sanguinis inter se multis coeuntibu' guttis
    ex aurique putat micis consistere posse
    aurum et de terris terram concrescere parvis,   840
    ignibus ex ignis, umorem umoribus esse,
    cetera consimili fingit ratione putatque.
    nec tamen esse ulla idem <ex> parte in rebus inane
    concedit neque corporibus finem esse secandis.

quare in utraque mihi pariter ratione videtur 845
errare atque illi, supra quos diximus ante.
adde quod imbecilla nimis primordia fingit;
si primordia sunt, simili quae praedita constant
natura atque ipsae res sunt aequeque laborant
et pereunt neque ab exitio res ulla refrenat. 850
nam quid in oppressu valido durabit eorum,
ut mortem effugiat, leti sub dentibus ipsis?
ignis an umor an aura? quid horum? sanguen an ossa?
nil ut opinor, ubi ex aequo res funditus omnis
tam mortalis erit quam quae manifesta videmus 855
ex oculis nostris aliqua vi victa perire.
at neque reccidere ad nilum res posse neque autem
crescere de nilo testor res ante probatas.
praeterea quoniam cibus auget corpus alitque,
scire licet nobis venas et sanguen et ossa 860

*

sive cibos omnis commixto corpore dicent
esse et habere in se nervorum corpora parva
ossaque et omnino venas partisque cruoris,
fiet uti cibus omnis, et aridus et liquor ipse,
ex alienigenis rebus constare putetur, 865
ossibus et nervis sanieque et sanguine mixto.
praeterea quaecumque e terra corpora crescunt
si sunt in terris, terram constare necessest
ex alienigenis, quae terris exoriuntur.
transfer item, totidem verbis utare licebit. 870
in lignis si flamma latet fumusque cinisque,
ex alienigenis consistant ligna necessest.
praeterea tellus quae corpora cumque alit, auget

*

ex alienigenis, quae lignis exoriuntur.
Linquitur hic quaedam latitandi copia tenvis, 875

id quod Anaxagoras sibi sumit, ut omnibus omnis
res putet inmixtas rebus latitare, sed illud
apparere unum cuius sint plurima mixta
et magis in promptu primaque in fronte locata.
quod tamen a vera longe ratione repulsumst. 880
conveniebat enim fruges quoque saepe, minaci
robore cum saxi franguntur, mittere signum
sanguinis aut aliquid, nostro quae corpore aluntur,
cum lapidi in lapidem terimus, manare cruorem.
consimili ratione herbas quoque saepe decebat 885
et latices dulcis guttas similique sapore
mittere, lanigerae quali sunt ubere lactis,
scilicet, et glebis terrarum saepe friatis
herbarum genera et fruges frondisque videri
dispertita inter terram latitare minute, 890
postremo in lignis cinerem fumumque videri,
cum praefracta forent, ignisque latere minutos.
quorum nil fieri quoniam manifesta docet res,
scire licet non esse in rebus res ita mixtas,
verum semina multimodis immixta latere 895
multarum rerum in rebus communia debent.
'at saepe in magnis fit montibus' inquis 'ut altis
arboribus vicina cacumina summa terantur
inter se, validis facere id cogentibus austris,
donec flammai fulserunt flore coorto.' 900
scilicet et non est lignis tamen insitus ignis,
verum semina sunt ardoris multa, terendo
quae cum confluxere, creant incendia silvis.
quod si facta foret silvis abscondita flamma,
non possent ullum tempus celarier ignes, 905
conficerent vulgo silvas, arbusta cremarent.
iamne vides igitur, paulo quod diximus ante,
permagni referre eadem primordia saepe
cum quibus et quali positura contineantur

et quos inter se dent motus accipiantque, 910
atque eadem paulo inter se mutata creare
ignes et lignum? quo pacto verba quoque ipsa
inter se paulo mutatis sunt elementis,
cum ligna atque ignis distincta voce notemus.
denique iam quaecumque in rebus cernis apertis 915
si fieri non posse putas, quin materiai
corpora consimili natura praedita fingas,
hac ratione tibi pereunt primordia rerum:
fiet uti risu tremulo concussa cachinnent
et lacrimis salsis umectent ora genasque. 920

21 LUCRETIUS' AIM (921-950)

Discard your prejudices
hear the rest with open ears.

I'm well aware
how obscure this stuff is.
I write because I must.
I'm ambitious – yes –
the legal high of praise
has its own attractions

but poetic inspiration spreads
like coloured water up through filter paper
leaving rainbow strata
in the fibres of my mind –

and most of all
because my verse gives power
to Lucretius' lonely ghost to walk again
in barefoot silence solitary ground
not skimmed by another's sole.

he's right behind,
when bold with joy I track the source
of springs my childhood never knew
taste the water, take samples
of the unrecorded species.

I wind myself a writer's wreath
from some aromatic new-world leaf
the ancient Muses never thought of using
to crown their poets.

so I choose verse – first because
it has the power to sever without pain

religion's knots that bite into the flesh
second, to make Lucretius' Latin shine
and put a surface gloss
on Life's dark complexity.

have you seen a doctor give a polio vaccine
to children? first they dissolve the serum
in some sweet liquid, and then the babies,
as yet unarmed against the hidden things
they'll find beneath appearance when they're older
listen only to their tongue
and swallow the whole lot down
caught out, not damaged – this time –
by adult desire to deceive, but rather
inoculated by such a simple trick.

so too, Lucretius' doctrine seems unpalatable
if you haven't tasted it
people are revolted by it
as by some strange smelly fruit
his Latin is difficult, impenetrable to most
not just because it's Latin
but because of what it says –
so I wanted, with these lines of honeyed song,
to detain you in the Eden of my verse
just long enough to show you
the star-draped body of the universe.

> nunc age quod superest cognosce et clarius audi.
> nec me animi fallit quam sint obscura; sed acri
> percussit thyrso laudis spes magna meum cor
> et simul incussit suavem mi in pectus amorem
> musarum, quo nunc instinctus mente vigenti   925

avia Pieridum peragro loca nullius ante
trita solo. iuvat integros accedere fontis
atque haurire, iuvatque novos decerpere flores
insignemque meo capiti petere inde coronam
unde prius nulli velarint tempora musae; 930
primum quod magnis doceo de rebus et artis
religionum animum nodis exsolvere pergo,
deinde quod obscura de re tam lucida pango
carmina, musaeo contingens cuncta lepore.
id quoque enim non ab nulla ratione videtur; 935
sed veluti pueris absinthia taetra medentes
cum dare conantur, prius oras pocula circum
contingunt mellis dulci flavoque liquore,
ut puerorum aetas improvida ludificetur
labrorum tenus, interea perpotet amarum 940
absinthi laticem deceptaque non capiatur,
sed potius tali pacto recreata valescat,
sic ego nunc, quoniam haec ratio plerumque videtur
tristior esse quibus non est tractata, retroque
vulgus abhorret ab hac, volui tibi suaviloquenti 945
carmine Pierio rationem exponere nostram
et quasi musaeo dulci contingere melle,
si tibi forte animum tali ratione tenere
versibus in nostris possem, dum perspicis omnem
naturam rerum qua constet compta figura. 950

22 THE UNIVERSE IS INFINITE (951-1051)

I've taught that the constituents of matter
flit like dust-motes in an ancient room
super-strong, untouched by time, though tiny:
come now, while I unroll the universe's text
to see if there's a limit to their number.

also that thing called Void –
that empty space that bodies move about in
does it have a boundary
where everything just stops?
or does it gape on endlessly?

the Things that Are don't end
for if they did, there'd been a no-man's-land
somewhere, between what is and isn't –
a fallow strip dividing
the universe from what's outside.

you must admit it's stupid
to say there's All, plus something more:
the universe has no boundary, can't be measured
it doesn't matter where you stand
in-finite is what stretches out around you.

if Space had edges – imagine standing
on that last overhang to Nothing
like an angler on the seamost rock:
you throw a stone; does its force of flight
arc glorious where you want?
or does it strike and fall, all that
potential wasted? You must admit
both possibilities exist.
but either way there's no escape for you:
you must dissolve the boundaries in your mind.

if there's something in its path
that forbids your lithoid drone
from carrying out its mission
or if you can throw it further – either way
you're not throwing from the end.

however far you go
wherever you put that Furthest Shore,
I'll be on your tail, demanding to know
what happens to your stone.
you can prove it to yourself
I already know the answer:
its flight-path will be empty far and wide
there's nowhere you can call the End.

our eyes tell us that things
draw borderlines round other things:
air hedges hills, and mountains air;
earth and sea draw maps around each other,
you can see the alternate shapes they make
in figure-ground reversal on the globe;
but the universe goes on without a limit.

what's more, if the universe was circumscribed,
corralled around by boundary fence
on which there's no dispute,
think of the vertical axis too:
if the cosmos had a floor
matter would ooze down towards it bit by bit
and everything under heaven's great marquee
would stop.

there wouldn't be a heaven, or a sun
because all that viscous matter would run like glass

slowly down an antique window-pane
thickening at the bottom.

but as things are, our molecules
have no down-time
there's no floor they can sit down on
and find their natural resting-place.
the world happens in a frenzy of activity
an infinity of particles rises up like smoke
from the abyss below.

on vertical and on horizontal planes
space is so big that not even a projectile
travelling at the speed of light
speeding the span of centuries
could cross it, nor in its headlong flight
make any less the distance left to go.

the universe extends
boundaryless through all dimensions.
this universe can never be
self-limiting – it's Void and Body placed
in endless alternation.

alterity creates infinity:
if Body didn't border Void, Void border Body
the world's bland changelessness
would just go on forever.
without this, neither sea nor land
nor gothic vaults of heaven
or mortal race, or tarnished bodies of the gods
could stand intact a single second.

matter would be blown apart
sucked away and vaporized
by some great vortex through the void
like a firestorm in a tunnel
or never formed at all.

the Primary Bodies didn't form a plan
put their heads together
and with due consideration
sign up to an agreement where to stand
and how to move: matter just mutates
in myriad motions for all time
assailed by blows.

this illusive order we call the universe
is just a sum of trial and error
a collusion of random motions
durable enough, though, once in place.
in a self-sustaining cycle
rivers feed the greedy sea
with generous cascades
cherished by the sun's warm heart
earth puts up flowers of living things
the sliding signs of heaven flicker into birth
matter without pause boils up from under
to restore what's lost.

just like when we're deprived of food
the soul runs out, and leaves only
the body's empty bag behind,
so the universe will bleed out
if matter diverts its course.
once it falls apart
no world can be forced back together

by squeezing from outside.
you might tamp down one part
jam it together with repeated blows
and wait for reinforcements to arrive;
but unless you bludgeon every part at once
wherever you slack off, matter bulges out
and takes what opportunity it finds
to bid for freedom.
so more must boil up all the time
to hold the universe together:
an endless flow of matter from all sides.

sed quoniam docui solidissima materiai
corpora perpetuo volitare invicta per aevum,
nunc age, summai quaedam sit finis eorum
necne sit, evolvamus; item quod inane repertumst
seu locus ac spatium, res in quo quaeque gerantur,   955
pervideamus utrum finitum funditus omne
constet an immensum pateat vasteque profundum.
omne quod est igitur nulla regione viarum
finitumst; namque extremum debebat habere.
extremum porro nullius posse videtur   960
esse, nisi ultra sit quod finiat; ut videatur
quo non longius haec sensus natura sequatur.
nunc extra summam quoniam nihil esse fatendum,
non habet extremum, caret ergo fine modoque.
nec refert quibus adsistas regionibus eius;   965
usque adeo, quem quisque locum possedit, in omnis
tantundem partis infinitum omne relinquit.
praeterea si iam finitum constituatur
omne quod est spatium, si quis procurrat ad oras
ultimus extremas iaciatque volatile telum,   970

id validis utrum contortum viribus ire
quo fuerit missum mavis longeque volare,
an prohibere aliquid censes obstareque posse?
alterutrum fatearis enim sumasque necessest.
quorum utrumque tibi effugium praecludit et omne 975
cogit ut exempta concedas fine patere.
nam sive est aliquid quod probeat efficiatque
quominu' quo missum est veniat finique locet se,
sive foras fertur, non est a fine profectum.
hoc pacto sequar atque, oras ubicumque locaris 980
extremas, quaeram quid telo denique fiat.
fiet uti nusquam possit consistere finis
effugiumque fugae prolatet copia semper.
postremo ante oculos res rem finire videtur; [998]
aer dissaepit collis atque aera montes, 985 [999]
terra mare et contra mare terras terminat omnis; [1000]
omne quidem vero nihil est quod finiat extra. [1001]
praeterea spatium summai totius omne [984]
undique si inclusum certis consisteret oris [985]
finitumque foret, iam copia materiai 990 [986]
undique ponderibus solidis confluxet ad imum
nec res ulla geri sub caeli tegmine posset
nec foret omnino caelum neque lumina solis,
quippe ubi materies omnis cumulata iaceret
ex infinito iam tempore subsidendo. 995 [991]
at nunc nimirum requies data principiorum
corporibus nullast, quia nil est funditus imum
quo quasi confluere et sedes ubi ponere possint.
semper in assiduo motu res quaeque geruntur
partibus <e> cunctis infernaque suppeditantur 1000 [996]
ex infinito cita corpora materiai. [997]
est igitur natura loci spatiumque profundi,
quod neque clara suo percurrere fulmina cursu
perpetuo possint aevi labentia tractu

nec prorsum facere ut restet minus ire meando; 1005
usque adeo passim patet ingens copia rebus
finibus exemptis in cunctas undique partis.
Ipsa modum porro sibi rerum summa parare
ne possit, natura tenet, quae corpus inani
et quod inane autem est finiri corpore cogit, 1010
ut sic alternis infinita omnia reddat,
aut etiam alterutrum, nisi terminet alterum eorum,
simplice natura pateat tamen inmoderatum.

*

nec mare nec tellus neque caeli lucida templa
nec mortale genus nec divum corpora sancta 1015
exiguum possent horai sistere tempus.
nam dispulsa suo de coetu materiai
copia ferretur magnum per inane soluta,
sive adeo potius numquam concreta creasset
ullam rem, quoniam cogi disiecta nequisset. 1020
nam certe neque consilio primordia rerum
ordine se suo quaeque sagaci mente locarunt
nec quos quaeque <darent motus pepigere profecto>
sed quia multa modis multis mutata per omne
ex infinito vexantur percita plagis, 1025
omne genus motus et coetus experiundo
tandem deveniunt in talis disposituras,
qualibus haec rerum consistit summa creata,
et multos etiam magnos servata per annos
ut semel in motus coniectast convenientis, 1030
efficit ut largis avidum mare fluminis undis
integrent amnes et solis terra vapore
fota novet fetus summissaque gens animantum
floreat et vivant labentis aetheris ignes;
quod nullo facerent pacto, nisi materiai 1035
ex infinito suboriri copia posset,

unde amissa solent reparare in tempore quaeque.
nam veluti privata cibo natura animantum
diffluit amittens corpus, sic omnia debent
dissolui simul ac defecit suppeditare 1040
materies aliqua ratione aversa viai.
nec plagae possunt extrinsecus undique summam
conservare omnem, quaecumque est conciliata.
cudere enim crebro possunt partemque morari,
dum veniant aliae ac suppleri summa queatur. 1045
interdum resilire tamen coguntur et una
principiis rerum spatium tempusque fugai
largiri, ut possint a coetu libera ferri.
quare etiam atque etiam suboriri multa necessest,
et tamen ut plagae quoque possint suppetere ipsae, 1050
infinita opus est vis undique materiai.

23 THERE IS NO MIDDLE (1052-1113)

Like a child, you think you're different.
you suppose that generations born before you
only knew a world where earth and man are central.

you're wrong: Lucretius' universe is no tame place
it's not held in by forces from outside
it doesn't stand there, either, on its own
parked midway by a stubborn tendency
towards some central point.

in his world there is no centre
no up, no sideways, no Antipodes
where people walk head-down
with arses in the air, zany reflections
of our more perfect lives.

forget that image of the earth
we all grew up with when
looking back to earth from space
you see half that friendly apple
swathed in night, half bright with day.

let your ideas fragment
your preconceptions stutter into silence

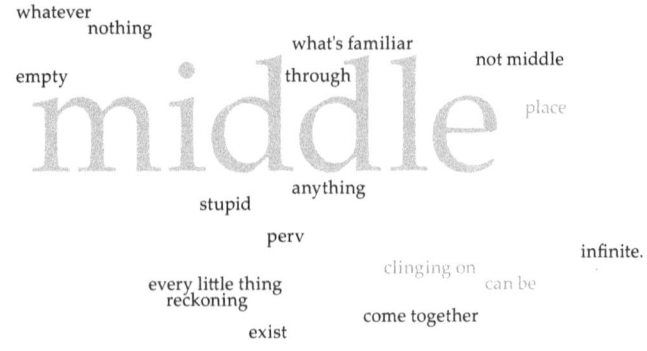

this universe has no boundary, no centre
it offers generous passage
wherever objects want to go.
the one thing they can't do is stop.
carried by trajectory alone
particles like tramps lack fixed abode
Void hustles them from place to place or else
they wander on according to their whim.
your longing for some middle ground is not enough
to cause them to set down their packs and join society.

the world is full of anarchy – just look around.
not everything aspires towards the middle.
things within earth's sphere of influence
might to the eye wrap round a central point:
lands and rivers, the sea's enclosing bubble
fed by mountain torrents;
but gamin fire and slender breath of air
strain like rebellious kids to break away
from parent sea and earth.

vagrant planets populate the universe
like fiery sheep put out to graze by shepherd sun:
no mediocrity can herd their souls together;
even trees must flout the laws of gravity
to suck up nutriment from soil
and turn it into flowers like Roman candles
fizzing from their tops.

Note: The archetype of the Latin manuscript is fragmentary at lines 1068-75 (see p. 112), with the result that the sense of these lines is incomplete, as though the words are hanging in space, as represented opposite.

if the universe hangs in balance, don't you think
its fragile treaty might one day be breached
the world's walls whoop away in flame-swift flight
sucked out by heaven's vortex
things vanish into space
like corpses through a jet's ripped fuselage
the earth withdraw beneath our feet as we
stumble though the universe's debris
till Void and Primary Bodies, dark to sight,
rule the silent world once more?

    illud in his rebus longe fuge credere, Memmi,
    in medium summae quod dicunt omnia niti,
    atque ideo mundi naturam stare sine ullis
    ictibus externis neque quoquam posse resolvi   1055
    summa atque ima, quod in medium sint omnia nixa
    (ipsum si quicquam posse in se sistere credis):
    et quae pondera sunt sub terris omnia sursum
    nitier in terraque retro requiescere posta,
    ut per aquas quae nunc rerum simulacra videmus.   1060
    et simili ratione animalia suppa vagari
    contendunt neque posse e terris in loca caeli
    reccidere inferiora magis quam corpora nostra
    sponte sua possint in caeli templa volare:
    illi cum videant solem, nos sidera noctis   1065
    cernere, et alternis nobiscum tempora caeli
    dividere et noctes parilis agitare diebus.
    sed vanus stolidis haec
    amplexi quod habent perv
    nam medium nihil esse potest   1070
    infinita. neque omnino, si iam
    possit ibi quicquam consistere
    quam quavis alia longe ratione

omnis enim locus ac spatium, quod in
per medium, per non medium, concedere 1075
aeque ponderibus, motus quacumque feruntur.
nec quisquam locus est, quo corpora cum venere,
ponderis amissa vi possint stare <in> inani;
nec quod inane autem est ulli subsistere debet,
quin, sua quod natura petit, concedere pergat. 1080
haud igitur possunt tali ratione teneri
res in concilium medii cuppedine victae.
praeterea quoniam non omnia corpora fingunt
in medium niti, sed terrarum atque liquoris,
umorem ponti magnasque e montibus undas, 1085 [1086]
et quasi terreno quae corpore contineantur, [1085]
at contra tenuis exponunt aeris auras
et calidos simul a medio differrier ignis,
atque ideo totum circum tremere aethera signis
et solis flammam per caeli caerula pasci, 1090
quod calor a medio fugiens se ibi conligat omnis,
nec prorsum arboribus summos frondescere ramos
posse, nisi a terris paulatim cuique cibatum

*

ne volucri ritu flammarum moenia mundi
diffugiant subito magnum per inane soluta
et ne cetera consimili ratione sequantur
neve ruant caeli tonitralia templa superne 1105
terraque se pedibus raptim subducat et omnis
inter permixtas rerum caelique ruinas
corpora solventis abeat per inane profundum,
temporis ut puncto nihil extet reliquiarum
desertum praeter spatium et primordia caeca. 1110
nam quacumque prius de parti corpora desse
constitues, haec rebus erit pars ianua leti,
hac se turba foras dabit omnis materiai.

24 THE WAY OF TRUTH (1114-1117)

My little work has led you on so far
truth's mountain stands before you now
a peak more daunting than Mount Sinai.
will you be brave enough to scale it in the dark?
you have to climb three thousand jagged steps
and all the while, with candle passed from hand to hand,
wick touched to wick in gentle kiss of flame,
a many-beaded ligature of light
will wind at last towards the summit.
so truth sets fire to truth
until we reach the top
and see the dawn.

      haec sic pernosces parva perductus opella;
      namque alid ex alio clarescet nec tibi caeca   1115
      nox iter eripiet quin ultima naturai
      pervideas: ita res accendent lumina rebus.

BIOGRAPHICAL NOTES

We know nothing substantive about TITUS LUCRETIUS CARUS. He is known only through his poem *De rerum natura* (On the Nature of the Universe), written c. 55 BCE. The poem is dedicated to one Memmius, probably Gaius Memmius, who was also associated with the 'neoteric' poets Catullus and Cinna.

Writing over four centuries later, the Church Father Jerome in his *Chronicon* retails a story, possibly apocryphal, that Lucretius was driven mad by a love potion and wrote the *De rerum natura* during intervals of sanity. This story probably arose from the quirky and often violent nature of the poem.

Lucretius is however a sublime poet, and the only extant epic poet of the Roman Republican era. His influence can be seen in all later Latin epics, from Virgil onwards. His poem became a major bone of contention after its rediscovery by the Renaissance humanist Poggio in 1417. It inspired both imitations and polemics, the latter particularly by Christian writers who took exception to Lucretius' astringent atheism, such as Cardinal Polignac in his *Anti-Lucretius* (1745).

EMMA GEE studied Classics at Sydney and Cambridge universities, lectured in Classics at the universities of Exeter, Sydney and St Andrews and is now a freelance Classical scholar, tutor and learning support assistant. Her most recent academic book, *Mapping the Afterlife,* combines ancient philosophy with modern music theory and psychology, and aims to present a thoroughgoing account of how the ancient afterlife functions as an exploration of the Self. She has also published academic works on Lucretius. Her translation of Lucretius' *De rerum natura* aims to make this astonishing and vital text accessible to new readers.

www.ingramcontent.com/pod-product-compliance
Lightning Source LLC
Chambersburg PA
CBHW022115090426
42743CB00008B/857